A JOURNEY TO FINANCIAL WELL-BEING

JESSE HARTMAN

DREAMS UNLIMITED

A Journey to Financial Well-Being
Copyright © 2008 by Jesse Hartman

Editor: Catherine Frenzel
Cover Design: David Hartman and Jesse Hartman
Logo Design: Scott Davidson
ISBN 978-0-615-25219-3

Published by:

Jesse Hartman
Dreams Unlimited
2274 Newport Way NW
Issaquah, WA 98027
206-817-3286
www.DreamsUnlimited.org

First Printing: December 2008

Printed in the United States of America

Dedication

I dedicate this book to those who
dare to dream
and never give up,
for this is the only
guaranteed path to success.

A Journey to Financial Well-Being

Table of Contents

Acknowledgements

You would not be reading this book right now if it were not for many people who have helped make this possible. First of all, I would like to thank God, as this came from a moment of inspiration at 30,000 feet on a cross-country flight in 2004.

I would like to thank my wife, Claudia Sanz de Santamaría, for without her continued love and support through all of my many failures over the years, I would not be who I am today.

Thank you to the many friends who have been very supportive and helped edit and provide valuable feedback to this book, especially Aaron MacCulloch and Jessica Smartt.

I would like to thank my mother, Karen Hartman, who has served as editor on several earlier versions of this book. Her tireless efforts have been quintessential in communicating the concepts in which the complicated becomes simple.

My father David Hartman and step-mother Diane Zimberoff have lived their lives in ways that have given me the greatest gift of all, confidence in myself and strength to live my life without ever giving up. Thank you for your leadership and wisdom.

A special thank you must be given to Scott Davidson, a friend, entrepreneur and genius with a computer. He has given much to this project and to the online website capabilities. Thank you, Scott!

In need of an editor, I received a referral by the best-selling author Tim Connor to his editor in New England. From the moment I contacted

Catherine Frenzel, I knew she was a perfect fit, and only hoped she felt the same. Through a wonderful collaboration and soft pushing from her, the manuscript was turned into the book you are about to read. Thank you, Catherine!

I would also like to thank everyone else in my life—family, friends, and colleagues—for the support and enthusiasm you have given me over the years. I credit much of my success to all of you.

And lastly, I would like to thank you, the reader, for without you there is no purpose writing or publishing this book. Thank you for buying it, thank you for reading it, and thank you for your continuing commitment to get up each day and reach for your goals as you live your live with courage.

Introduction

Welcome to *A Journey to Financial Well-Being*, your next step to creating more of the life you want. Wherever you are in life, and however little you think you have, this book is the perfect next step. It combines education with simple systems and strategies that you can begin using immediately to begin elevating your financial health. This is not a "get rich quick" book, and will not give you any stock tips on the next tech megalith.

You may be familiar with the parable, *If you give a man a fish, he eats for a day. If you teach a man how to fish; he will eat for a lifetime.* That is the purpose of this book: to give you the resources and teach you how to make the necessary financial decisions in your life to get where you want to go.

The last thing I want to do is offer advice and tell you what to do. That is akin to helping someone get out of a financial mess, but not teaching them how to avoid getting back in it in the future. Without the resources and education, most people will keep repeating the cycle over and over.

Let this be your first step in a new direction, a direction of change, a direction toward what you want in life with the confidence that you can and will get there. I have found that successful people are like anyone else, except that they constantly learn, course correct, and never give up. It is as simple as knowing where you want to go, creating a plan to get there, and beginning to execute the plan, one step at a time.

With that, I wish you well, and hope you find great value in this book. It was created through my own financial failures, from which I learned the most valuable lessons.

Enjoy!

PART I

HOW DID WE GET INTO THIS MESS?

Chapter One

What I Learned From
My Biggest Financial Failure

To introduce you to this book, it will help to better understand my story, how I came to write this. This book—in many ways—is my story, and I am excited to share it with you.

I have always been a magnet to money. My mom still tells the story of me being the cashier at age three when she sold pears out of the back of her pickup. Although I don't remember this, I do remember a hundred other ways I was involved in making money in my youth.

At age five, I wrote, typed, illustrated, published, and sold a story door-to-door. I also collected aluminum cans and newspapers from the neighborhood for extra money. I had a lemonade stand, sold magazines, and sold candy and gum to students during recess and at summer camp.

Upon graduating high school, I became infatuated with traveling and my dream came true. I spent a year studying abroad in France. It was my first time living away from home, managing my money, and I wanted to make sure that it would last. I surely didn't want to go hungry or have to leave early.

I kept a financial journal, writing down every transaction at the end of the day. My theory was that if I kept a record of everything, I would have all the information in case I figured some system to manage my money. That is exactly what happened. From a daily journal of my transactions, I began a more sophisticated approach.

I would add it up every week to see how I was doing. Sometimes I needed to slow down my spending and sometimes I had a little extra. It was a simple system that helped me to manage my money.

Sixty days after graduating college, my girlfriend and I drove to Florida for a six-month internship she had with Walt Disney World. During this time, I researched a business opportunity in the vending industry and took the plunge.

In August 2001, we maxed out $40,000 on our credit cards and three days later, 75 vending machines arrived at our apartment doorstep in cardboard boxes. We assembled, placed, located, filled, and monitored our new business.

It was a disaster from the very beginning.

By January 2002, when we returned back to Seattle, we had all the experience with vending machines that we thought possible or ever would want. One machine had a rat infestation, and another was stolen. Several were infested with ants, and one was actually chewed to pieces by rodents of some kind—to the point that it was completely destroyed. Many locations decided that they no longer wanted to have our vending machines. We had gone from a dream to a nightmare. In addition, we had a negative monthly cash flow in Florida due to our low salaries and inability to live on such a modest income. We had accrued many thousands of dollars of credit card debt from subsidizing our monthly income.

We owed $50,000, most of which was on our credit cards.

My girlfriend and I were staying in my friend's garage-turned-guest bedroom, wondering what on earth had happened, how it had happened so quickly (only six months), and what we were going to do about it.

What I Learned from My Biggest Financial Failure

I found a job and don't have to tell you that with taking home $1,900 per month in an expensive city like Seattle, it was very difficult to make our $750-minimum credit card payments.

We finally got our vending business up and running in Seattle.

We were so far in debt that some friends suggested we declare bankruptcy, since it seemed impossible to imagine paying off all the debts we owed. I could not bring myself to declare bankruptcy and decided that, one way or another, we would find a way to pay off everybody we owed.

Somehow, in the midst of all this, my girlfriend saw potential in me that I could not—and married me. This was the greatest moment of my life, and the turning point I credit with much of my life's success.

Shortly thereafter, we received a coupon in the mail for a discounted $400 financial plan through a reputable international financial planning company. Although we didn't have the $400, we charged it on a credit card in hopes that our troubles would finally be solved by the financial expert.

Two weeks after our initial two-hour visit, we had our second appointment where our advisor gave us an expensive leather binder with a 200-page financial plan. We left feeling more distraught than before. The summary of 200 pages was to spend the next ten years of our lives repaying our debts without traveling, vacationing, buying a home, starting a family, or dining out. To us at age 23, this felt like a death sentence.

After a couple of weeks in despair, a day arrived when I felt especially inspired and decided once for all to rid myself of debt. I sat down with pen and paper to devise a plan to find a way out of the hole I had created. My plan designated set amounts per paycheck that would go directly to pay our debts, in addition to the modest income we received from the vending machines. The plan, when finished, would take us only four years to climb back to the level we were at when we graduated. That plan, in short, meant devoting most of our income to repaying our debts, with a small amount of money set aside for fun and for our future dreams.

We have modified this plan many times since September 2002. For years, we reduced our debt by over $1,000 per month.

Four years later, we had a net worth of over $150,000, and were completely debt free! We bought our first home in August 2004, one year ahead of our goal.

When I sat down in September 2002 to create a financial plan, I also created a savings feature as part of the plan. In the beginning, we saved a set amount from every paycheck towards our goals of traveling, giving to our favorite charities, etc. By allocating $50 per paycheck, being committed, and consistently saving for over a year, we were able to have the amount we needed for a four-week trip to Colombia to spend with my wife's family. None of this would have been possible without a plan, and the discipline to follow it.

You can do anything you commit to, with a plan of action, and the discipline to continue living it. I am proof that this is possible.

I wonder if my success would have happened had I not purchased 75 vending machines and reached such a desperate point. It feels good to have crawled out of that financial hole and be able to share my experiences with you, so that you, too, can achieve all that you truly deserve.

The Talmud says, *A happy man is one who is content with what he has*— a definition I embrace, since it empowers each of us to choose it as a paradigm. A new way of thinking that allows one to feel the abundance of great wealth, in this moment, and on our own personal journey to greater financial well-being.

Chapter Two

It's Never Too Late to Take Action

Do you feel as though it's too late for you to create greater financial well-being and enjoy life like the "beautiful" people on TV? Maybe you feel you don't have what it takes, are not smart enough, not educated enough, don't have enough time or are too deep in debt. Excuses will never go away; and whether you decide to start today or in ten years, there is one thing that we know for certain will happen. In ten years, you will be ten years older than you are today, whether you plan for it or not.

Think about yourself ten years ago. Did you ever imagine that you would be where you are today? Probably not. The reason you are where you are today is because you created it, first through your thoughts, then your words, then your actions—then there were results, your life. Life is a great teacher, but only if we are ready to listen and learn.

There are those who talk and those who take action. The ones who take action get things done, move forward, and make many mistakes along the way. They learn from these mistakes, so that their future actions are done by making wiser decisions. This is called wisdom.

Those who talk in lieu of taking action may not fail, may not make any mistakes, but they will fail to move in any direction. The inertia of inaction will keep them comfortably thinking of how they want it to be and not making it happen.

Action is the only path to success. Reading this book is a great action step. *What you do with the knowledge from this book*—not the knowledge alone—will determine your results. I encourage you to take action and move boldly into the direction of the future you desire!

The action steps below and throughout this book are part of the journey that will guide you to your next steps in creating more of what you want in life. Simply skipping past them will only prevent you from gaining the full benefit from this book. I urge you to take some time and complete each action step before moving forward.

Action Steps:

Journal about the fears that keep you from moving forward and your vision of the life you are in the process of creating. What keeps you from taking action and what can propel you into action?

For example: *My past failures keep me from taking action because if I fail again, I just don't think I can handle it. I am afraid of what others might say and think of me. However, my dream of having three-day weekends and supporting my family without my spouse having to work drives me into taking action!*

Commit to completing this book and taking action for at least 30 days. This will spring you toward the future that you are now creating.

Nothing limits achievement like small thinking; nothing expands possibilities like unleashed imagination.

William Arthur Ward

Chapter Three

Welcome to Life's Classroom

So you want more money and greater happiness. Who doesn't want to win the next mega-million lotto, or find the new get-rich-quick idea? I have spent a lot of time, energy, and money seeking riches. I have found that most people who try to succeed financially usually do not. Often they are using the wrong systems, not committed, not sufficiently motivated; or having that much financial success is too far out of their comfort zone. People sabotage themselves to avoid the fear of financial success, or spend all of their lottery winnings and end up right back where they were—so very comfortable in their original comfort zone.

This is not a get-rich-quick book, but it is filled with educational tools for anybody who wishes to have a higher quality of life and greater wealth. Some may do this more quickly, others over a longer period of time. Either way, financial success is not only possible, but easier than you may think when you have the right tools, systems, attitude, and commitment.

We are where we are because of everything we have been exposed to. Our beliefs (what we know to be true) and habits are what got you and me to where we are right now. The most effective way to have a different experience in the future is to change the beliefs and habits that you exhibit today. This, combined with systems for success, an unwavering commitment and action, can change your life forever.

This entire book is meant to educate, empower, enlighten, and foster inspiration so that you can get up every day and do the things you must do to achieve the results you want in your life, financial and otherwise.

For best results and greater success, take notes, read this aloud, for you will retain more if you use more of your senses. Review this frequently; and whenever you feel frustrated and powerless, come back to this resource and review the information as well as your notes. It will give you great inspiration and keep you moving in the right direction.

Action Steps:

Journal about experiences in which you have learned valuable lessons. What beliefs do you still hold onto that limit you, holding you back from success? Why is it more important to be right about these beliefs than letting them go and believing in something that will empower you, thrusting you toward that which you say is most important. This will help you better understand why you believe, think, and act the way you do, in addition to providing valuable paradigms that may need to be shifted in order to make room for greater success.

For example: *I started a business with $50,000 that failed. What I learned from this experience was not to trust myself in making decisions. Over the years, I have learned that I can benefit from seeking the guidance of others close to me. I have also learned that something too good to be true, usually is. These have been invaluable lessons.*

Watch your thoughts, for they become words.
Watch your words, for they become actions.
Watch your actions, for they become habits.
Watch your habits, for they become character.
Watch your character, for it becomes your destiny.

Frank Outlaw

The only thing I would add is at the beginning: that our beliefs become our thoughts. Whether we are aware of them or they are unconscious, they are the foundation of who we are and what we are capable of. Without fully understanding and changing the beliefs that are self-limiting, we can go only as far as our beliefs will allow.

Chapter Four

The American Dream/Nightmare

For thousands of years, humans have lived in groups, clans, and extended families—until the Industrial Revolution.

We are taught that the Industrial Revolution was the greatest innovation in modern history, leading to the great achievements we have today of modern technology (i.e., everything that is assembled by people, computers, or mechanically—which would be just about everything). What we are not taught is that, for the first time, families were separated in massive numbers throughout the world as men moved away from home to work in the factories to support their families.

We gave up our independence for a paycheck, and have been less and less independent ever since. We have been working for a paycheck for well over a century now, and in this time, have become more and more dependant on our employers, the government, and others for our financial stability.

At what cost was the Industrial Revolution a success, and for whom was it successful? Millions of boys, girls, men, and women worked in conditions and for durations that are now illegal and done only in Third World counties. We call them *sweat shops* and expose companies that continue to use these cheap labor tactics for their own profit. For the masses that were not educated, there were very few options.

Thankfully, there were advocates and, eventually, laws were passed to protect workers in the United States. Labor laws created the 40-hour work week and regulations against child labor abuse. We take these for granted today, but it was our great-grandparents who banded together to bring about these changes.

Between the Industrial Revolution and World War II, families began to change significantly. Once consisting of several generations living under one roof, they began thinning to single-family households that are now all that we know.

World War II came and all the able-bodied men joined the fight, leaving the factories in great need of workers. Women entered the workplace. After WWII, many women did not want to leave their jobs and, over the decades, more and more women began working.

In the 1950's, the average family in America had one car, mom stayed home and dad worked. One income afforded the family everything it needed. There may not have been much left over, but they were part of the middle class and had a higher quality of life, spending time together, and enjoying natural exercise. The greatest present any child could dream of was a bicycle.

In the 1960's, hippies rapidly changed society and culture, rebelling against the order and structure of previous generations.

By the 1980's, the baby boomers realized that they had a good 40-50 years left and would be well-advised to make better plans or they really would be living the rest of their life in ways they no longer wanted to live. The baby boomers hit the corporate floor running. The 1980's was a decade filled with tremendous corporate growth as the boomers went from Woodstock to Wall Street. They also settled down, got married (many for the second time) and began having children.

The 1990's was a decade of great financial growth and the birth of the Internet. The children of the baby boomers began growing up and became contributing members of society during a period of great wealth. What was the experience growing up for these 60 million children? How was it different from their parents?

The term *latchkey kid* did not exist until this generation arrived. There were 60 million children, but no parents to be seen. They knew that they had parents because they received expensive gifts at Christmas and for their birthdays, but they spent little time with their parents.

The dual-income family, working to climb the corporate ladder, changed the priority of our society from family first to career and money first. With half of all families ending in divorce, the single parents had no choice but to work. But that's okay; they would buy a nice gift to make up for their absence at the Little League games, plays, and other activities. Love was communicated by the presents and lavish lifestyle their parents provided, with computers, TV's, cell phones, Internet, their own car at age 16. Do you remember Harry Chapin's song *Cat's in the Cradle and the Silver Spoon*? He wrote this song in 1974, singing about the major changes in society that have only increased with time.

This is why a baby boomer's son or daughter at age 20, moving away from home for the first time, expects to live a lifestyle equivalent to their parents who have worked hard for over two decades to achieve it. What did they achieve? The boomers may have money—if they didn't lose it in the dot.com crash, or spend it all on the latest and largest SUV. Many children of the boomers never had to work for their toys, and learned that families were less important than money and careers. Actions speak louder than words, and the entitlement of 20 years of met expectations led to even greater expectations of entitlement.

Since they can't afford the lifestyle they want on their $10.50-an-hour job, they buy the "love and acceptance" (things they previously received from mom and dad) on their credit cards. This is aided by corporations marketing how their product will make them popular, loved, and accepted, the quintessential elements on Maslow's hierarchy of human needs. *You can buy it with payments as low as....* And, voila, you're hooked. Because what people want most in life is to be accepted and loved. They subconsciously believe—after a few million commercials, billboards and radio ads—that "it" will bring the answer to life's un-fulfillment. But, in reality, it brings nothing more than a larger-than-expected credit card bill in 30 days.

It worked so well with the children of the baby boomers that it also worked on everyone else in society. Here we are in the year 2008, overextended, overworked, overstressed, and unfulfilled. Is this the American Dream or the American Nightmare?

Action Steps:

Journal about your life. Are you living the *"American Dream"* or the *"American Nightmare"*? What are your values, and how can they guide you to the future you are now creating? Are they aligned with your actions? Understanding your values is foundational to success. Our values are what our lives are built upon.

Example: *I value integrity, honesty and freedom—the basis from which I create what I want in life. I choose to act only in ways that foster this within me in and around me. If I stray, I will course-correct as soon as possible.*

For more information on learning about your values and their importance in your life, see Dr. Stephen Covey's book *The 7 Habits of Highly Effective People.*

---

*There are three constants in life...
change, choice and principles.*

Dr Stephen Covey

Chapter Five

It's Not *What* You Want, But *Why* You Want It

This is the point at which I tell you that this book is not about money. That's right, it's not about money. It is about what you desire from money. It is about what you want to do, the experience you want to have, and how you would contribute to the world. The real question is not *what* you want, but *why* you want it. *What* you want is much easier to answer than *why*. When you answer *why*, you will know what experience you are looking for.

There is great power behind the answer to this question. Nobody wants money just to have it. The reasons most people want money is for what they believe it will provide them: food, shelter, security, education, fun, love, acceptance, safety, time with family, traveling, power, etc. Money is not really anybody's desire, even though we say it out loud every day and think it hundreds of times daily. What we want are all the great things we believe it will buy. Money is the most likely vehicle to those things.

Behind each of these reasons is the foundation of what brings us joy in life, and will be different for each person. For example, the driving needs in my life are connecting with others, contributing to a sense of greater well-being, sharing adventure, embracing change, and seeking excitement.

By learning enough about myself to know that these driving needs are my foundation, I now know *why* I want to travel (adventure and excitement), spend time with my family and friends (connecting with others), and why I am writing this book (contributing to a sense of greater well-being).

Knowing this about myself, I can choose to create and embrace these driving needs regardless of my financial wealth. This is where the *why* and the *what* come together and meet for the first time. Having a lot of money will not suddenly give you the answers to life's questions. It is in the process of self-discovery, the final frontier, where we find out what joy is and how to create more of it.

I have said for many years that money rarely creates happiness, but it can help sustain a life of true wealth—the wealth of love, joy, and true fulfillment. It is only when we discover within ourselves the magic that lights our fire, that brings the music within to the surface, that we can use financial wealth to create even more and begin to share it with others. It is the energy of life.

The truth is, money is a form of energy, and energy is in constant motion. If you tried to conserve your energy and lay in bed without moving for a month, you would become ill, physically uncomfortable and acquire bed sores. The same thing happens with money. It comes and goes, and our sense of financial well-being depends on both movements.

Wealthy people are no different than you or I. Some are happy, while others are unhappy. Those who experience the greatest joy are grateful for the same things you are. They just have more of it: time with loved ones and friends, really delicious food, living comfortably, flying first class, sleeping in, traveling, and a really good cup of coffee on a rainy day.

One habit the wealthy tend to excel at is focusing on what they want or desire. The more they focus on it, the more they bring it into existence. Focus works for the working class and the poor, too. The poor think about how they are going to pay their rent and afford groceries, and the end result is, they spend all their time tending to these thoughts. The middle class thinks about paying their children's college education, buying newer cars, going on vacation and paying their credit cards. The wealthy think about how they will increase their cash flow, grow their wealth and spend more time doing what they truly enjoy, whatever that is. The result, regardless of what you think about, is that you will focus your time, money and energy turning those thoughts into reality.

For the action steps of this chapter, think about the experiences that you want, the things you want to own, the people you want to spend time with, and places you want to travel that are waiting for you. What excites you? What do you desire with enough intensity that you are willing to turn it into a reality?

Action Steps:
Journal about your life. Are you living the *"American Dream"* or the *"American Nightmare"*? What are your values, and how can they guide you to the future you are now creating? Are they aligned with your actions? Understanding your values is foundational to success. Our values are what our lives are built upon.

Example: *I value integrity, honesty and freedom—the basis from which I create what I want in life. I choose to act only in ways that foster this within me in and around me. If I stray, I will course-correct as soon as possible.*

For more information on learning about your values and their importance in your life, see Dr. Stephen Covey's book *The 7 Habits of Highly Effective People.*

Create a personal collage of the future you are in the process of creating; the more creative and vivid, the better. This will help create a destination, and your subconscious can begin working towards its achievement.

I recently heard an interview with a successful man who had done this exercise. Years later, he found his collage and realized he was living in *"the* house" whose picture he had cut out of a magazine and put in his collage. The power of putting what you want out into the universe is limitless.

As a second action step, get out a piece of paper and answer the following question. Answer it over and over and over again, until you cannot think of another possibility. Completing the college first may help you in this exercise. When you are done with all possible answers, you will have a rough draft of your driving needs, which are the experiences you are looking for and continue to create in life in one form or another.

The question: What experience are you looking for?

Its choice—not chance—that
determines your destiny.

Jean Nidetch

Chapter Six

Standard of Living vs. Quality of Life

What is *standard of living*? The concept of *standard of living* has been used far too long to compare you and me with the Joneses in an attempt to get us to spend more money to buy things we probably don't really need in the first place.

For the purpose of this book, I will define *standard of living* as how we keep score in America: He who has the biggest SUV, most expensive looking clothes, or largest home has the highest standard of living.

Although this is typically true, I wish to redefine *standard of living* as the amount of time devoted to survival; in other words, how much time you spend making money to support your lifestyle.

I will define *quality of life* as the amount of time spent doing what you love.

Most of us spend 40, 50, or even more hours per week devoted to survival. There are tribes in many areas of the world that continue to spend as little as three hours a day on survival, and the rest of their time is spent on pursuing what they love to do.

This is a very important concept to understand because very few people enjoy their work so much that they would do it for free. For the other 99.9%, there is work and there is life—and seldom do they meet as a joyous union.

Standard of Living vs. Quality of Life

Do not confuse these two concepts. Madison Avenue would like you to believe that purchasing the latest in fashion or the newest cell phone will bring you greater quality of life. After the endorphins fade, the only thing left is a credit card bill.

Which is more important to you? It is sometimes a hard choice to say *no* to the things we think we want; but saying *no* to what is not important allows us to say *yes* to what is important.

You can become debt free, save and invest for your future, and still afford what is most important. I have done it and will show you how to do it, too.

It starts by prioritizing your life. What is most important to you? Do you ever forget to get gas for your car and find yourself on the side of the road, or forget to eat until you find yourself emaciated and without strength? I didn't think so. Why is it that we manage to accomplish these things, but forget our wedding anniversary, or our children's basketball game, or to save $100 per month?

Priorities! Whatever has the highest importance and urgency will always get done.

Did you ever procrastinate in high school and/or college? Do you remember the weekend before a term paper was due and suddenly getting very motivated to spend the next 48 hours preparing, researching, writing, editing, and finally turning in a beautiful assignment? That was a very low priority in the first eight weeks of the quarter—until three days before it was due, when it shot up to number one.

That is how life works. What has the highest priority gets done. Priorities can change instantly. One minute, you are working with a valued client—a very high priority. The next minute, you receive a phone call that somebody you love is in the hospital—your priorities immediately change and your very valued client suddenly seems to pale in importance.

What is a priority? I define a *priority* as something of importance. What we choose to make a priority will determine both our standard of living and our quality of life.

My wife and I recently discussed some of the most enjoyable times in our lives, and realized that they all had some things in common. We were very busy, doing things we loved to do. We were surrounded by other people also choosing to do the same things. Our lives felt very balanced. Because we were so busy, we had to prioritize and choose what to do and not to. TV was a passive activity that we chose not to do. We enjoyed watching TV, but when we prioritized all of our options, TV was often moved to a very low position on our list of priorities.

We choose to eat together sitting down at our dining room table, enjoying our nourishing meal and each other's company. We sit down every week and have a family meeting where we review the previous week and plan and prioritize the one to come. I like the feeling of clarity that I feel, knowing what we aim to accomplish before we begin the week.

I encourage you to look at where you choose to spend your time. How much time do you spend commuting, at work, watching TV, being with your family and loved ones?

Are you leading a balanced life? I encourage you to look at the areas in your life where you are the most uncomfortable. That is probably where you are least balanced. I know it is hard to face, but the benefits of a balanced life, time with loved ones, a profession one is proud of, and great health is the quality of life everybody desires.

Action Steps:

Think about your standard of living and the quality of your life. How would you rate each one in your life?

Standard of Living (scale 1-10: 1 is lowest, 10 is highest)

    1   2   3   4   5   6   7   8   9   10

Quality of Life (scale 1-10: 1 is lowest, 10 is highest)

    1   2   3   4   5   6   7   8   9   10

Have a discussion about this with your family.

Decide what is most important and focus your energy on those things. If you find that you spend a lot of time doing things that are not important (such as watching TV or playing video games), decide to reallocate that time for something more important.

The key is not to prioritize
what's on your schedule,
but to schedule your priorities.

Dr. Stephen Covey

PART II

YOU ARE A BUSINESS

Chapter Seven

You Are a Business

Did you know that you are a business?

Webster's unabridged dictionary defines *business* as *the purchase and sale of goods or services in an attempt to make a profit.*

Do you sell your time (services) to an employer for a specified amount of money? If you answered *yes* to this question, then you are a business. Like a business, you have income and expenses and pay taxes. The other half of the definition is if you *attempt to make a profit.* Do you intend to have money left over when your expenses are paid? Answering this question may help you understand if you are a business or a charity!

Most people go about managing their money with the paradigm that if there is money, it should be spent; and if there isn't any money, that it's okay to borrow money for the desired expense.

Can you imagine running a business with this paradigm? How long do you think it would take before it would go out of business? You may have heard that 9 out of 10 businesses fail. The reason this occurs is that 9 out of 10 people start a business and run it like they do their personal finances.

This is the American paradigm, and may be the one you are currently using. If it is, you may wish to change it for one that will provide a greater sense of financial stewardship for yourself and your family.

You Are a Business

For those of us who sell our time to an employer, ask yourself what your time is worth. Regardless of the amount of money you receive in compensation from your employer, you are selling your time, the one and only nonrenewable resource, your most precious commodity.

Income is probably the only part of a business that most people track— in a checkbook, or simply looking at their pay stub on payday to see how much they earned for the pay period and for the year. "Wow," you might think, "I earned so much money this year. Where did it all go?"

Expenses are the area where most people get into trouble. Do you know where your money goes? How much do you spend monthly on groceries, dining out, and gas?

Monitoring both income and expenses is crucial to business and your personal finances. Remember, you are a business. Without knowing where your money is coming from or going to, how can you adequately plan for the future?

We will go into this in more depth in Chapter 14.

Action Steps:

Look at your life as a business, owned by you. Who are your clients? (Remember, your clients are your employer and other sources of income). Are you happy working with them? If you wanted to work for different clients, what kind would you choose? Would your role with them be different than it is currently?

Get out your journal and begin answering these questions. Remember, you are the business owner. You own your time and your money, two very valuable assets. How will you choose to invest them in the future?

Accept responsibility for your life. Know that it is you who will get you where you want to go, no one else.

Les Brown

Chapter Eight

Financial Statement

The first step of planning where you want to go is finding out where you are right now. In your journey to financial well-being, this will be your financial statement, your first step toward a greater sense of financial well-being.

A financial statement, in its simplest form, is a list of your assets minus a list of your liabilities. At the end of this equation, you will find your net worth.

To ensure that everyone reading this fully understands these terms, we will define *asset* as anything that currently has a positive financial value. *Liability* will be defined as anything that has a negative financial value.

For example, your car's asset value is what you can sell it for (e.g., $13,000). The liability of your car is what you owe the bank (e.g., $15,000). That means that your car has a negative net worth (asset minus liability) of -$2,000.

Your first exercise is to fill out your first financial statement. A blank financial statement is provided at the end of this chapter for you to fill out.

Under the asset category, list everything you possess of value—e.g., savings account $500, Toyota Camry $10,000, 401K $3,500, home $300,000.

Financial Statement

Under liabilities, list all the money you owe, with the dollar amount of each item—e.g., Bank of America Visa $3,650, car loan $18,580; debt from medical bills, student loans, mortgages, lines of credit, personal loans and any other debt or loan that you have.

When you are done, there will be a total for both sides of the financial statement (assets and liabilities). If your assets are more than your liabilities, you have a positive net worth; and if your liabilities are more than your assets, you have a negative net worth. There are many different ways of measuring and evaluating your financial wealth. I recommend updating this financial statement monthly to track your progress. You will be amazed as you watch your financial success and see your progress every month over the years.

My Financial Statement			
Assets		Liabilities	
Description	Value	Description	Value
Total Asset Value		Total Liabilities Value	
Current Net Worth			

Congratulations on your first step toward greater financial well-being! This step is hard for many people. It may have been the first time that you have written down your assets and liabilities.

Financial Statement

Was the result of your financial statement different than you thought it would be? Do you see more clearly how each side of the statement affects your net worth? The first financial statement I ever did (at age 23) showed that my net worth was a negative $50,000! Although this was hard to face, it helped motivate me to take action where necessary to create the changes I wanted.

Action Steps:

Go to www.DreamsUnlimited.org and find *My Financial Statement*. Download it (it's free) and fill it out. Update this monthly, so that you can watch your progress and be a good steward of your financial future. [1]

Money is one of the most important subjects of your entire life. Some of life's greatest enjoyments and most of life's greatest disappointments stem from your decisions about money. Whether you experience great peace of mind or constant anxiety will depend on getting your finances under control.

Robert G. Allen

---

[1] If you are unable to access the Internet, you may photocopy any chart from this book (see Appendix II) or send me a request with an S.A.S.E. (business size) and I will send you one copy of each spreadsheet free of charge. Send your request to Jesse Hartman, Dreams Unlimited, 2274 Newport Way NW, Issaquah, WA 98027 If you will be doing the charts manually, without using a computer, I highly encourage you use a calculator to speed up the process and ensure accuracy.

PART III

SPENDING LESS

Chapter Nine

Why Spending Too Much Is the Real Problem

Overspending is epidemic in the United States. There was an excellent PBS special titled "Affluenza" that débuted in the late 90's. It was followed by a successful book by the same name. In this book, the authors define *affluenza* as *a painful, contagious, socially transmitted condition of overload, debt, anxiety, and waste resulting from the dogged pursuit of more.*

As discussed in the first section, American culture has changed a great deal over the last century. Many factors have combined to create the culture we live in today, one in which we are taught to be good consumers, that an economic downturn can be solved by buying more stuff.

In April of 2008, Economic Stimulus Checks were mailed to millions of Americans with the expectation that the $600 received by the average family would be spent on consumer products to boost the economy. Polls showed that those with lower incomes spent more of this money than did those with higher incomes, who tended to save their money.

This is a case in point, demonstrating that those with a better understanding of basic financial principles value having money in the bank during hard times. It may not stimulate the economy, but it will help keep a family solvent.

Why Spending Too Much Is the Real Problem

The reason there was a need to "stimulate" the economy was due to the overspending of Americans in the sub-prime real estate markets, buying houses they simply could not afford. Spending our way out of a financial problem is a paradigm that simply is not a long-term solution.

Today we have more stuff than we will ever need and most of it we no longer even desire. I have become very adamant in recent years that I wish to receive no gifts at Christmas time. Instead, I ask that in its place a gift be given to those in need. I even joked last year that I would invite everyone I knew to my home and let them take anything they want.

There are many great works about this subject (see www.Dreams Unlimited.org). I wish to show the impact of affluenza on our society and, most likely, on you. My wife and I often joke when one of us is about to buy something we do not need, saying, *"Does someone have affluenza?"*

Affluenza is a challenge at the heart of what is required to create a greater sense of financial well-being. It is a constant challenge for me that I continue to face daily, reminding myself frequently, "What *is most important in my life? Is this going to help me achieve it*?"

This is why choosing where to spend our money is such a great challenge. Like food, there are ways of spending money that will create financial heartburn and obesity (indebtedness), as well as greater financial vitality and well-being.

Changing one's diet to healthier foods and beginning to exercise is a lot like changing one's financial habits and financial exercises. These changes do not occur overnight, and it not an easy path; but the benefits are so great that the short-term challenges faced in the transition are of little consequence.

Why Spending Too Much Is the Real Problem

Disposable income

When you are paid, there are two numbers that you probably look at: the larger amount next to the words *gross income* and the smaller amount next to the words *net income*.

Gross income is the total amount you earn. If you worked 40 hours and earn $10 an hour, your paycheck will indicate that your gross income is $400.00.

However, the government learned long ago that the best way to get taxes is to collect them from you before you ever get your paycheck. Listed below the gross income is where you will find the taxes, Medicare, and social security taken out of your paycheck. This amount is anywhere from 20%-40% depending on your tax bracket and other factors.

The amount you get to deposit into your bank account is your net income: gross income minus these taxes.

The amount you have left over after paying your bills is what is referred to as *disposable income*. This is the amount that everybody—you and your vendors—wants a piece of. This is where most people get into trouble, spending what is left over without thinking of where they are going and the most effective way to use that money.

It's not about getting more money

Have you ever said to yourself, *"If I could just get that raise, that new position, earn an extra $5,000 a year…"*? Almost everybody believes that earning more is the answer to their problems. Have you ever received the raise, new position, or extra money? Was it the solution that you had been waiting for? Most people will begin spending their raise the day they learn of their future increase in pay.

Why Spending Too Much Is the Real Problem

Americans, on average, spend about 102% of their total income. That means if you earn $20,000 a year, you will most likely spend about $20,800 a year; and if you earn $100,000, your spending will be approximately $102,000 per year. Regardless of income, most families spend more than they make.

Can you see that this is a problem? These families probably have no financial plan, and many people will not be retiring at any age, let alone realizing their dreams of enjoying life like the wealthy do.

Everybody wants to experience the benefits of wealth, but few are willing to do what the wealthy do to create wealth.

The system of wealth

There is a system created by the wealthy and paid for by the poor and the middle class that keeps wealth in the hands of the few.

It is really quite simple: Wealthy people buy assets, and the poor and middle class buy liabilities.

The financially savvy buy something of value that will continue to increase in value—e.g., a rental house, antique car, art work, or a business. Take the example of a rental house. It is purchased and immediately rented out to a family in need of a home. See below for details:

Purchase Price, $100,000
Monthly mortgage, property taxes, and insurance, $1,000
Amount received in rental income from renter, $1,200
Positive monthly cash flow, $200
Annual increase in the value of the rental house, $6,800[2]

---

[2] 6.8% annual equity growth according to the National Association of Realtors, based on a national average from records kept since 1968.

Why Spending Too Much Is the Real Problem

The bottom line of this example is that the person who bought the house and rented it out is making $200 per month, and his/her investment is increasing in value by an estimated $6,800 in the first year.

This is an example of how the wealthy buy assets that will continue to grow in value and, in many cases, put money in their pocket.

The other end of this investment is the middle-income family that is renting the house. By renting, they are helping the owner earn $200 a month and a nice annual equity appreciation. However, the family living in this house is getting no financial benefit from living there.

Think about this from two perspectives. First, the perspective of the middle-class consumer who works hard all week and then goes out on Friday night, visits the mall on Saturday, and enjoys his new car on leisurely Sunday afternoon drives. This person, probably leasing his car, will have a car payment for the rest of his life, will work hard for the money that he spends and will stay in this cycle for the rest of his life, always waiting for Friday at 5:00 p.m. to spend his money.

The second perspective is from the person who owns the restaurant/bar that is packed every Friday night, or the owner of a shop at the mall, or the owner of the car dealership where the person in the example above purchased his car. These people also look forward to the weekend because they will earn a lot of money from the middle class spending money at their establishments.

Wealthy people create and buy assets and use their money from that to invest in more opportunities and gain even more money.

In 2006, the poor and middle class spent 102% of their income making others wealthy!

The solution is to join the wealthy. This book is your next step in gaining the understanding and knowledge to begin making decisions that will increase your financial well-being.

Action Steps:

Play the following prosperity game alone or with your family. It is fun and gets your mind thinking in a way that will serve you in creating greater financial well-being.

Find a way to generate revenue of $1,000,000 in the next 12 months. Use pen, paper, and calculator. This is a game, and you can be as crazy and creative as possible. The purpose is not to actually generate $1,000,000, but to get your mind thinking in a way it is not used to, thinking outside its boundaries or comfort zone.

Example: If I wanted to generate revenue of $1,000,000, I could sell smoothies. If I sold smoothies for $5 each, it would take 200,000 smoothies to generate $1,000,000. How would I sell 200,000 smoothies? I could have a small smoothie stand by the beach every Saturday and Sunday. If I could sell 100 smoothies each day, I could generate $1,000,000 in about 19 years. That's a long time....

How about I sell a product online... maybe a cookbook... and sell it for $19.95. If I wanted to generate $1,000,000 in revenue, I would have to sell 50,125 books. How would I do that? If I sold them online and was listed on Amazon and in all the bookstores, I might generate 25 sales per month (just a guess), which would be 200 per year. If I sold them on my own website and generated 1,000 new hits every day, by giving out a recipe of the day, and sold 5 daily, that would be another 1,825 per year. I need only 48,000 to go. I've got it... I will get it into the hands of Costco members. Due to their large volume, I may sell 1,000 per day and it would take only 48 days to reach the million dollar mark. Yea, I win!

This is an enjoyable game, for which the purpose is to think creatively, have fun, and use your mind in ways that exercise under-used areas to help you create greater financial well-being.

We can't solve problems by using the same kind of thinking we used when we created them.

Albert Einstein

If you want to create greater financial well-being, you must think differently than you have thus far in your life!

Chapter Ten

How to Save $500 to $50,000 a Year

Since one of the largest problems today is overspending, learning to live within one's means is a wise habit to learn. In this section, I will provide you with many ways to save hundreds of dollars every month.

This topic can bring up uncomfortable feelings for some people. You may be feeling that you will have to give up everything that you find enjoyable in life in order to have more money. Although you may choose to spend your money differently, the only pressure you will face will be from yourself. Give up any resistance you may have and read this chapter with an open mind.

Cutting back is sometimes necessary, but using strategies that cut costs while maintaining quality of life is possible. If you have any money-saving strategies that are not listed here, please email me at jessehartman@yahoo.com and I will add them to the Resources section of my website, www.DreamsUnlimited.org. You will sleep better knowing you made a contribution that helped others around the globe create greater financial well-being.

Imagine that you were an investor looking to put some venture capital into a business. Would you look for a business that is spending future profits on fancy furniture, high salaries, and going into debt to do it? Or would you look for a business where the management team works for very little to keep costs to a minimum so that every dollar earned can go back into the business to make it grow even larger?

I think you know the answer to that question. If it is that obvious, then why do so many people spend their earnings on liabilities (anything that will not grow in value) and businesses go out of business because money is spent before it is ever earned.

How do you know if you are living within your means? A good way to know is if you can live off the cash you earn without using a credit card. If so, then you are spending less than 100% of your earnings and are, therefore, living within your means.

It is a skill necessary to master before building a business or gaining significant wealth. Mastering the skill of "simple living" now, will prepare you for wealth that will come to you in the future. The average American household in 2006 spent 102% of their income, regardless of the amount of their earnings. That means they spent more than they earned, whether they brought in $20,000 or $500,000.

By the way, most people who win the lotto spend or lose it in a year or two and end up further in debt than before they won. If they had mastered the skill of simple living, spending within their means, they may have made different decisions in how they spent their money.

There are many ways to save money without giving up your lifestyle. Many of these techniques you may begin implementing immediately, but many will require that you look at your Monthly Cash Flow (see Chapter 15).

30 Ways You Can Begin
Saving Money Today

1. **Buy subscriptions to magazines or newspapers that you buy regularly in stores.**
   a. Benefit: You will often pay up to 70% less than the cover price you would pay in a store.
   b. Savings: $5-$40 per month, $60-$480 per year

2.   Frequent the public library.

   a. Benefits: free DVD's, CD's, books, books on CD, hundreds of magazines, newspapers in many languages, lectures, computer classes, and education!
   b. Cost of a library card? Priceless!
   c. Savings: $4.00 per week, $208 per year (based on 1 DVD per week)
   d. Savings: $1.00 per week, $52 per year (1 magazine per week read at the library)

3.   Make shopping lists.

   a. Make lists for everything you intend to buy. Shop only for what you need and avoid shopping as recreation, for this is a great temptation to overspend.
   b. Savings: thousands of dollars

4. Buy only what you need, nothing more.

   a. When you buy something, go in, get it, and get out!
   b. Keep your receipts. Sometimes you come to your senses after you get home. You can always go back and return it later.

5. Take a lunch to work.

   a. Make extra for dinner and take the leftovers to work the following day. Take a sandwich, carrots and a V8 or juice from home instead of buying it at work. You will save money and eat much healthier.
   b. Savings: If you can save $5 per day by taking lunch to work, you save $792 per year.

6. Use an Entertainment Book.

   a. We were given an Entertainment book as a gift by our financial planner (schools and Scouts also sell them as a fundraiser), and it became an annual gift we gave ourselves. We have saved hundreds each year from the coupons in this book.

b. We have saved $60 at Safeway, at least $100 on movies, and $100-$200 on dining out.

c. Cost of Entertainment book, $35

d. Total potential savings: $260 if all coupons are used.

e. Savings: at least $225 per year

7. Eat/drink out or see movies during designated times for lower pricing.

c. Most restaurants have happy hour when drinks and food are half price.

d. Savings: $50 per month, $600 per year dining out during happy hour, and/or using dining coupons

e. Matinee movie prices are discounted several dollars before 5 p.m.

f. Use coupons to go at peak times, but pay matinee prices.

g. Savings: $4 per month, $48 per year on going to the movies— per person.

8. Wash your car at home.

a. Buy a hose, a car-washing brush and some soap and save money today!

b. Savings: $10-$50 per month, and $120-$600 per year.

9. Buy cheaper gas.

a. Scout out the gas stations with cheaper gas prices.

b. Visit websites—e.g., www.gasbuddy.com—where you can search by zip code to find the cheapest gas prices.

c. Savings: $3.75-$7.50 per month, $45-90 per year based on saving 5-10 cents per gallon

10. Eat before you go out.

a. You will buy far fewer groceries if you eat before food shopping, not being tempted by your growling stomach.

b. Eat before you go to the movies and save on popcorn and drinks at absurd prices.

c. Eating a healthy meal at home, prior to going out, will allow you to enjoy your outing, and not get caught eating fast food simply because it is quick. Fast food costs add up quickly.

d. Savings: $20-100 per month, $260-$1300 per year

11. Make your morning coffee at home instead of buying one at Starbucks.

a. $4 per day 240 working days a year is $960. That is a lot of money! Do you know how much coffee you can buy at the store and make at home for the same price? About 96 pounds worth of coffee. My guess is about 1,875-2,500 cups of coffee, or almost a 7-year supply of coffee at home.

b. Savings: $60-$70 per month, $720-$840 per year

12. Shop during sales, clearance, seasonal times, or at off-price divisions.

a. Every season, the clothing stores gear up for their new fashions and have huge discounts on their previous clothing that they want to sell urgently.

b. Outlet stores and off-price branches of some high-end stores always offer signature high quality at a lower price.

c. Plan on using some of your money for the times that you can predict will be good for buying things—such as Black Friday (the day after Thanksgiving) or the after-Christmas period between December 26 and January 1 every year.

d. If you buy everything discounted 50%, you spend $500 and just saved yourself $500.

e. Instead of buying the Coach purse, think about going to JC Penny's.

f. Savings: $45 per month, $500 per year—at least!

13. Get rid of credit cards with an annual fee.

    a. What benefit would a credit card give somebody that costs $85 per year?

    b. Will the benefit be greater than the $85?

    c. It is usually a waste of money unless you pay no interest, and rack up 30,000 frequent flyer miles or more per year.

    d. If your credit is such that this is the only credit you can get, use it to build better credit so that you can upgrade to better cards—if you need them at all.

    e. Savings: $25-$150 per year plus the interest

14. Set the timer on your furnace and air conditioner for the time you are at home.

    a. We chose not to heat or cool our home when we were not home and it made a big difference in our monthly electric bill.

    b. Savings: $5-$75 per month, $60-$900 per year

15. Buy fewer things, but of superior quality.

    a. Buy products of superior quality so you don't have to replace them frequently.

    b. For example, cheap shoes that cost $30 may last for only six months, while shoes for $100 may last for one, two, or even several years.

    c. Savings: $10-$25 per month; $120, $300 per year

16. Pay insurance annually or semi-annually.

    a. There are discounts for insurance payments made in advance—$5, $10, $15 or more.

    b. Savings: $5-$50 per year

17. Split the garbage bill with a neighbor if you have extra room in your garbage can.

    a. I know somebody who saved $10 per month ($120 per year) by doing this.

    b. Savings: $5-10 per month, $60-$120 per year

18. Pay less for TV and Internet.

    a. Go from 200 channels to 50 or 25. Watch the savings grow.

    b. Internet can be as cheap as FREE if you live in a city with free wireless. If you don't, then you can find it for at least as low as $10 per month. How much are you paying?

    c. VOIP companies such as Vonage offer great rates on phone and Internet.

    d. Savings: $10-$125 per month, $120-$1500 per year

19. Look for food coupons.

    a. Look in the paper, the mailbox or online for coupons for the grocery store.

    b. Seek out 2-for-1 coupons for the restaurants you wish to visit, or visit the ones that have the 2-for-1 discounts. Save 50% off dining out.

    c. Savings: $5-100 per month, $60-$1200 per year

20. Buy music online for $1 per song instead of $18 for the entire CD.

    a. Especially if you like only one song.

    b. Savings: $17-$85 per month, $204-$1,020 per year

21. Reduce postage.

    a. Pay bills online and eliminate the 30 postage stamps for the 30 bills you send monthly, plus the cost of envelopes and checks.

    b. Savings $8 per month, $96 per year

22. Always ask if there are discounts for students, military, AAA or AARP members.

   a. Discounts on movies, hotels, air travel, insurance, dining, and so much more

   b. Savings: $100 or more annually

23. Set up an appointment with an accountant to see if the/she can save you money.

   a. It could be the best money you have ever spent.

24. Use the gym at your apartment community—it's FREE!

   a. Savings: $10-$100 per month; $120-$1,200 per year

25. Find FREE banking

   a. When you put your money in a bank, they are lending it out and earning up to 20% interest on it. Why pay a bank to borrow your money?

   b. Often credit unions offer better rates and cost less than traditional banks.

   c. Savings: $5-$20 per month, and $60-$240 per year.

26. Quit smoking—it's expensive (not to mention, deadly)

   a. Visit www.lungs.org/ccs.html to calculate how much you can save.

   b. Savings: $150 per month, and $1,800 per year, (based on 1 pack a day at $5.00)

27. Stop buying lotto tickets.

   a. It is a cheap way to buy some hope that you will win it big—but you won't.

   b. Savings: $20 per month;,$1,040 per year, (based on $5 per week)

28. Cook for the month, one-stop.

a. Dinners Ready and Cookin' Dinners are companies where you can go to cook meals for the month. They prepare everything for you, and even help you cook. You pay about $200 for 72 single-portioned meals, less than $3 per meal, and spend only 2 hours cooking!

b. You will save additionally because you will dine out less frequently due to this convenience.

c. If you enjoy cooking, there are online sites and cookbooks such as *"Once a Month Cooking"* that will provide you with recipes that will last—saving you time and money.

d. Savings: $50-$500 per month, and $600-$6,000 per year

29. Drive an older reliable car for FREE

a. Buy an inexpensive older car outright and have no payments (save hundreds per month).

b. Pay only for gas and insurance.

c. Don't worry if it gets scratched.

d. Savings: $100-$1,000 per month, $1,200-$12,000 per year

30. You can live rent-free!

a. Many small apartment communities are owned and managed by individuals or small companies. They often will give you a free apartment in exchange for vacuuming the hallways, and being available after work to show vacant apartments to people looking to rent. Big savings, little work!

b. Savings: $500-$1,500 per month, and $6,000 to $18,000 per year

**Total savings from this list alone is
$50 - $4,123 per month!
$600 - $49,476 per year!**

As you can see, there are many resources available to save money. The ones I tend to highlight the most are the library, vehicles, and rent.

The library is an amazing resource that people under-utilize. Besides local newspapers, the library carries DVD's, videos, music, CD's, and audio-books. Not only is it free, but you can search the catalog from home using the Internet, and order the books and DVD's you desire. Librarians will help you find anything that you are looking for. The library also has computers to access the Internet and free computer classes in Word, Excel, and other programs.

Cars are the area in which I think more money could be saved than anywhere else. The auto industry has done an excellent job of convincing us that we need to be driving the newest car. In fact, most millionaires when asked, purchased a two-to-three-year-old luxury sedan and drove it for ten years before repeating the process. They understand that the vehicle is a liability and the least amount of money should be spent in this area.

A reliable car can be purchased for as low as a few thousand dollars or $100 per month. When you are done making these minimal payments, you own it. That means your liabilities go down and you have extra money to allocate to something of greater importance.

Above you saw over 30 ways of saving money, some in small ways and some in larger ways. If you want to get on the fast track, look at the greatest impact you can have. Forget saving $8 a month on stamps and sell your car for one that is more economical with better fuel efficiency.

Some people love their cars. Remember, everything you see here are only suggestions. If you derive that much pleasure from your car, by all means keep that car payment. I, however, get much more satisfaction from having greater financial well-being than from driving a new car.

Lastly, make lists so when you go shopping. You need three new, white, men's dress shirts. See what's on sale or wait until there is one, and then take advantage of it. Even travel can be done at discount prices.

For example, expedia.com, hotels.com, and most credit cards offer some kind of special discount when you use them. Don't be impulsive unless it really is something that you need right now and it can't wait.

If you follow these guidelines, you will rarely pay retail and you will save thousands every year.

Action Steps:

Make a commitment right now and choose one way in which you intend to save money for the next 30 days. Take action and write it in your agenda, or use a sticky note on your desk that will remind you daily of this commitment. Thinking is not enough. Action, action, action!

Visit www.DreamsUnlimited.org for more ideas and resources to save money,

---

Self-discipline is when your
conscience tells you to do
something, and you don't talk back.

W. K. Hope

Chapter Eleven

The Truth about Debt

The average person in the United States has over $7,500 in consumer credit card debt and that number has been rising over the last decade! For most of the middle class, debt consists of credit card, car, student, and mortgage loans. Just about everybody has first-hand experience or knows someone struggling financially due to debts they have accrued.

When do you use your credit cards? When you hand the cashier your MasterCard, are you thinking of how you will pay off the bill? Can you afford what you are buying without the credit card?

On a recent trip to Bogotá, Colombia, I saw an interesting system. When one hands their credit card to the cashier in Colombia, the cashier asks how many payments they would like to pay off the purchase. That's right; the consumer must decide before the purchase how long they will take to pay off the purchase amount. Can you imagine a cashier in America asking you such a personal question before your purchase?

What shame in saying anything other than one payment, indicating that you can't afford to pay it off when the bill comes. Perhaps that is what we need, or something like it, because the credit card companies will stop at nothing to get you hooked on more and more debt until you spend the rest of your life making them rich.

If we went back in time 100 years ago, we would see a very different social paradigm concerning debt and borrowing money. It was not only frowned upon, it was virtually a sin, akin to selling one's soul. As the decades passed, a new generation felt it appropriate to borrow money only for a home since it was an investment, and in those days (1950's) the average household expense on housing was approximately 17% of the household income, whereas today it is closer to 35% - 50%, as seen with the recent foreclosure of millions of homes across the country.

As time went on, a new generation came of age with the dawning of the credit card, otherwise known as the Diner's Card, soon followed by the Bank Americard. This new generation began borrowing a little more money for cars and other expensive items, but it was not looked upon favorably.

With each new generation, debt became more and more of a social norm, accepted by society, until now it is shocking to find someone who chooses not to use debt when making a purchase. We live in the only country on the planet where you can go to the pet store, buy a puppy using store credit, and have it repossessed when you fail to make your payments.

Let's take a second look at our relatives 100 years ago. Why didn't they borrow money? Banks wouldn't lend money without significant collateral, such as real estate. If someone owned their own home free and clear, they could potentially lose it if they couldn't pay back the loan to the bank. They probably spent most of their life saving every penny to afford to purchase their home, and they weren't about to gamble with it.

The only other option in borrowing money was from someone in a dark alley in the middle of the night. You could borrow money with little or no collateral because the fear of physical harm to the borrower if payment was not received, was usually enough to ensure full payment.

Borrowing money was viewed as gambling, and everyone knew it was a foolish game, that the house always wins, and the risks were too great to go down that road.

The Truth about Debt

When people borrow money, they become subservient to the lender, regardless of whether it is a credit card, family member, or the bank. Borrowing money changes a relationship significantly and immediately. The owner of the note becomes the master, and you, the servant. It is a harsh reality, but oh so true. All you have to do is look at the millions of people today who are forced to work more hours, year after year, to make the increasing payments on their various loans: cars, homes, credit cards, and other debts they now find themselves in.

Understanding this paradigm of overspending for immediate gratification is the first step in the process of changing one's financial future. Going from a paradigm of instant gratification to one of pay-as-you go is simple, but not easy. I make a special note here that many challenging things in life may be simple, yet very difficult. We all know that we should spend less and save more, eat less and exercise more—yet getting over denying ourselves and loved ones what we/they want is very challenging, and is the very main reason why the United States has so many people who live paycheck to paycheck.

Yet, it is worse now than ever before because now living paycheck to paycheck means keeping up with the minimum payments on all of the various debts that have been accrued. This cycle is stressful, but at least 100 years ago they broke even at the end of the day, and did not have to worry about anything they had being repossessed.

Each time you make a conscious choice to take on more debt, you are making a choice to become a servant to the owner of your loan, until it is paid in full.

There are other theories, thoughts, and paradigms about borrowing money. Several recent authors, speakers, and well-known specialists on the subject of personal finance and getting rich have a different paradigm than the one I've just described. Some believe that it is okay to borrow money as long as it is for the sole purpose of making more money, such as a loan for a business or investment.

The Truth about Debt

A prime example of this is borrowing money to purchase real estate using leverage and other people's money to make a profit. The concept is simple. Find a house that is undervalued, use the least amount of your own money in the form of a down payment and borrow as much as possible from the bank in the form of a mortgage. Then flip the house, selling it in the near future, or rent it out. Although you can find great returns in this type of investment, there are no guarantees.

There will be over 2,000,000 foreclosures in 2008. Why? Because many people thought they could afford something that, in the end, they really could not. Millions speculated on the market and gambled with their credit and other people's money. The market changed, companies went out of business, people across the country were laid off, and prices plummeted. As of this writing, housing prices in Southern California have dropped in half in several areas most affected by the most recent downturn in the market.

Can you imagine purchasing a home for $600,000, and two years later, it being worth only $300,000? What if you have to move, relocate, or experience a financial hardship and must sell? Millions of people are experiencing that right now.

I'm not saying this always happens, because in actuality, real estate has been a very strong investment. What I am saying is that there is risk in every scenario of borrowing money, whether it is from your brother-in-law, the bank, a credit card, or refinancing your house. Investment opportunities that require you borrow money should be thoroughly researched with special interest in risk analysis. Had I done that, I would have never ended up $50,000 in debt on my credit cards with nothing to show for it but 75 vending machines.

Debt is debt, whether it's making you money or not; whether it's in the form of credit cards, a car payment or anything else. Any money you owe someone else is keeping you from experiencing greater financial well-being.

The Truth about Debt

If you knew how free it feels to be debt-free, would you make different decisions? The world opens up to you with so many new options. I have heard from many people after years of indebtedness and finally becoming debt-free, how light and liberated they feel. Suddenly, the second job is not necessary. The most precious commodity is time, and that is the one thing that everyone wants more of. Becoming debt-free is the best way I know to get more time in the long term, although in the short term, you may lose time attempting to pay off your creditors.

Freedom of choice is a beautiful thing and I encourage you to embrace this new paradigm, for it is and has been used by virtually all of the self-made millionaires in the United States, who seldom use debt, and tend to live in simplicity with regard to their choices in spending money. How do you think they became millionaires in the first place?

I end this chapter with the story of Sears and Roebuck. As you know, Sears has been around for over 100 years. A few decades ago, they entered the business of lending money, and it quickly became their most successful department. It grew and grew and in the 1980's, when Sears was faced with great financial hardship, they sold their financial services division, also known as the Discover Card, for several billion dollars. Sears made more money lending money than they did selling their products. They learned that there is more money in lending money than anything else. What a valuable lesson.

Regardless of the reason you chose to borrow money, pay it off as soon as possible and begin enjoying the liberating freedom of living debt free. See Chapter 13 for a step-by-step approach to getting out of debt and stay debt free!

Action Steps:

Review the liabilities side of the financial statement you did earlier. Look at the way you view debt, and the ways in which it has impacted your life thus far. Decide how you would like to change the way in which you use debt, and read the following chapters to learn how to get out of debt and stay out forever!

You cannot escape the responsibility of tomorrow by evading it today.

Abraham Lincoln

Chapter Twelve

Credit Card Secrets

How would you like to earn a 1,000% return on your investment? If you invested $100 at that rate, a year later you would have $1,000. Let me demonstrate.

Currently, if you deposit $100 in a bank, a year later you will have about $102 (a roughly 2% increase). When you put $100 into the bank, the bank gets to loan your $100.00 to somebody else and charge them 20% interest in the form of auto or home loans, or credit cards. That means they will earn $20 every year on your $100, and give you only about $2 of that. That is a great deal for the bank, but how about you? Are you happy getting that split, $2 for you and $20 for the bank?

Have you noticed that many companies such as Starbucks, Disney, Barnes & Noble, Amazon, Banana Republic, and others have credit cards now with "special offers"? They are trying to entice you to sign up and use their cards. Some offers include 10% off your total purchase the day you sign up, special discounts, or airline miles. Did you know that department store employees get a commission and bonuses for each credit card they get somebody to sign up for?

The store pays a bonus for each new credit card, plus the special offer they give you, and then starts reaping the benefits: the interest you will pay on the sofa, clothes, books, or coffee you purchased last month with your new credit card. So, you will pay it off over the next month or two or three...or 36, or 72, or 150. The longer it takes you to pay it off, the more money they earn.

The credit card industry can afford to have over 20% of all cardholders file for bankruptcy and still make money. They make money on volume, knowing that most people will pay it back, nice and slowly, paying high interest rates and penalties if the limit is exceeded or the payment is received late.

Don't you wish you were the bank? If you are thinking this isn't fair, *think again.* There are always two sides to a coin. Yes, banks make a tremendous amount of money and are in the business of using your money to earn their money. That is how they stay in business.

I developed strategies that helped me use credit cards to get out of debt, and even earn money. I was able to use the rules set by the credit card companies to become debt-free by using credit cards in my favor.

If you are like most people, you get at least one offer daily for a new credit card at a low or even 0% APR (annual percentage rate). The credit card company is hoping that you open a new account, max it out, and in a couple of months when your low APR increases to 18%, you will start making them rich. This is what most people do, and that is why you get daily offers for new cards. Turn the tables and make this work for you! The offers are opportunities for you to go shopping for the best interest rate.

If you are offered a low APR for 6-12 months for balance transfers—or, even better, a 0% APR on balance transfers and purchases for 6-12 months—you can take this opportunity to reduce the interest rate on your higher-interest credit cards by moving your debts to this new card. *The tricky part is creating a system to remember when it will increase to 18%.* In Chapter 14, you will find the system I used to become debt-free.

I used this method with over $40,000 in debt and never had an APR above 4.9% over the three years it took to pay it off. I recommended this strategy to a client who had almost $200,000 on his credit cards. By using this strategy, he was able to save over $3,500 per month in interest alone.

According to a recent speech from Suze Orman, 1/3 of your FICO[3] credit score is made up of the ratio of your debt to available credit. What this means is that a low ratio of debt to available credit will increase your FICO score, which is used by insurance companies to determine your premiums, and by employers to determine if they want to hire you. In short, your FICO score has a great impact on your life, whether you apply for a loan or not. For example: John has $5,000 of debt he owes on one credit card and three other credit cards that are empty, but have $5,000 each of available credit. That means he has $5,000 of current debt and $20,000 of total available credit, or a 25% ratio of debt to credit. If he were to cancel the three credit cards that are empty, his ratio of debt ($5,000) to credit ($5,000) would be 100% and that would have a dramatically negative impact on his FICO Score. It is important to maintain a low ratio, and cancel credit cards only when it will have little effect on the FICO score.

Did you know that paying off your credit card by paying only the minimum payment will often take over 30 years? It takes this long because the $100 minimum payment is going mostly to interest. Imagine that you owe $5,000 on a credit card. Of your $100 minimum monthly payment, $80 is going to interest and $20 is going to pay your principle, reducing the amount you owe now to $4,980. At this rate, it will take you over 20 years to pay off this credit card and you will have paid a whopping $24,996!

If you have a 0% APR, all $100 gets applied directly to your principle, reducing your debt to $4,900. The difference between becoming debt-free in a few years (paying $5,000-$6,000) and becoming debt-free in 20

---

[3] FICO stands for Fair Isaac Corporation and was founded in 1956 by engineer Bill Fair and mathematician Earl Isaac. They developed the FICO scores to measure credit risk. Today these are the most used credit scores in the world. FICO scores are available through all major consumer reporting agencies in the United States including Equifax, Experian, and TransUnion.

years (paying almost $25,000) is simply using the system you will find in the following chapter.

Lastly, I want to address credit scores. Your credit score is one of the most valuable and important tools in creating greater financial well-being. I sometimes call it my financial integrity. It calculates the likelihood that one will pay back money when borrowed. The lower the number, the less likely it is that the bank will be repaid; the higher the number, the more likely it is that the bank will be repaid.

If you have a higher credit score when you apply for a loan (house, car, etc.), you will have a lower interest rate from the lending institution. However, the lower your score, the higher your rate of interest. Lower scores translate into payments that can be as high as double those of someone with a high credit score.

Having a high credit score can save you many thousands of dollars every year, and provide you options that are not available to those with lower credit scores.

Action Steps:

Get your credit score from all three credit bureaus: TransUnion, Experian and Equifax. The following website provides a free annual credit report by all three agencies: www.annual creditreport.com.

---

*Creditors have better memories
than debtors.*

Benjamin Franklin

Chapter Thirteen

How to Get Out of Debt

The hybrid stacking method

The following is the formula that I used to get out of debt and start building wealth.

Use the following steps with the spreadsheet at the end of this section to establish your plan to eliminate all of your unhealthy debts.

Step 1—Stop accruing unhealthy debt. If you use a credit card, it MUST be paid off in full when you receive the bill.

Step 2—Make a list of all your consumer debts. This would include credit cards, department store cards, car loans, school loans, and any other debts that are outstanding.

Step 3—Next to each debt listed above, make 3 columns:
- Amount owed
- Interest Rate of loan
- Minimum monthly payment

Step 4—The goal is to pay off your debts, and of course, pay as little interest as possible, right? Take the debt that you have with the highest rate of interest and find a way to decrease it.
You can do this by simply calling the financial institution and telling them that you have a better offer from XYZ Company and that if they are unable to give you a better interest rate, you will move your loan

elsewhere. More often than not, they will oblige you with a better interest rate, since it is preferable to get a little interest from you than none at all.

If this does not work, hang up, call back, and speak with someone else. You will frequently find that most representatives will offer you something different. Keep calling until you get what you want.

If, after several calls, they do not offer what you are looking for, simply look at your other credit cards that are empty. Often times, they will give you a good rate if you transfer your balance to their financial institution.

Depending on your credit, you may be eligible for some of the great credit card offers that you receive in the mail every day. Look at the fine print before charging into it. You want to save money, not end up with just another credit card with a high rate of interest.

(Someone who didn't read the fine print found out the hard way that when she was accidentally late on a payment for her new 0% card, it automatically defaulted to the 18% APR.)

You may also combine your debts. If you owe $2,000 on one credit card, and $3,000 on another, you may be able to combine them both into a larger $5,000 amount. This will simplify your accounts.

Do this with all of your debts. Try to decrease the interest rate on every one as much as possible. This gives you more leverage in paying them off. More of the money you were paying before you did this will apply to the principle and thus reduce your debts more quickly.

Step 5—Make a list with 4 columns
- Column 1—Who you owe (e.g., Bank of America Visa Credit Card)
- Column 2—How much you owe (e.g., $3,200)

- Column 3—Interest rate of debt (e.g., 6%)
- Column 4—Minimum monthly payment (e.g., $85)

Step 6—Put a 1 next to the debt with the highest interest rate. Put a 2 next to the debt with the next highest interest rate until you have them all numbered. The last number should be your debt with the lowest interest rate.

Step 7—Pay the minimum payment on all of your debts except the one with a 1 next to it. For that one, you will pay the minimum payment plus an additional specified amount that you can commit to every month.

It is important to commit additional money—$100 per month or as much as you can afford—to reduce this debt. The extra money will be a large factor in the time it will take you to pay off all of your debts. You will budget a specific amount to spend monthly on debt payments and it will be a fixed expense.

Step 8—When debt number 1 is paid off, continue paying the minimum payments on your debts except for number 2. Number 2 will now get the minimum payment you were paying previously, *plus the entire monthly amount* you were paying toward number 1. It will take much less time to pay off number 2.
When number 2 is paid off, continue this pattern until they are all paid off. You should pay the same amount every month from when you start this debt-reduction program until your last payment.

Step 9—Now that you are debt-free, continue to commit this monthly amount toward growing your net worth. Put it in a savings account, buy a house, or pay off the one you have even faster. But commit to use this money for the purpose of your financial future.

	My Debt Freedom: The Hybrid Stacking Method				
Rank	Debt owed to	Amount Owed	Interest Rate	Minimum Payment/Mo.	DebtFree Date

Additional Action Steps

Some other practical things you can do are:

1. **Stop buying things that are not necessary.**

   Think very hard before purchasing an item. How important is it for you to have it right now? Will the quality of your life be diminished if you don't buy it? I do this when I find toys I want to buy for myself. The other day, I bought a web cam thinking I had to have it. When I got home, I started thinking about it some more and finally decided that I would rather spend that $85 on something else. So I took it back to the store and got my money back.

2. **Make a list and shop only for those items.**

   We have a master list on our fridge. When we get low on anything in the kitchen, we write it down. We also write down anything else we "need" from other stores—such as socks, shoes, pens, a stapler, toothpaste, etc. This helps us be effective by visiting only the stores we need to, so we save time. We also save a great deal of money by buying only what we need and not wandering around other stores tempting ourselves with things we don't need and don't know we want because we haven't seen them.

Wherever you are on your financial journey, I recommend you educate yourself more and seek professional assistance with a financial planner. I compare finances to exercise. If you want to run and do well in a marathon, you will need coaching, practice and a plan. The same applies to your finances.

Action Steps:

If you have any consumer debts, make sure that you complete the above activity if you haven't already. It is the most effective way to become debt-free. You can download *My Debt Freedom* for free at www.DreamsUnlimited.org.

Credit is a system whereby a person who can not pay gets another person who can not pay to guarantee that he can pay.

Charles Dickens

Chapter Fourteen

Monitoring Income and Expenses

If you use the tools that I am giving you, within 30 days you will be able to see where your money is going, and decide if that is how you want to continue spending your money.

Today you will begin using the program, *My Money.* When you take the first step towards your goal immediately after you make your goal, you are ten times more likely to accomplish it. Let's get started.

Step one is to begin keeping a receipt for every single dollar you spend. At the end of every day, input the information from your receipts into the *My Money* program. You will also enter any income you earned—from your paycheck, commissions, cash for babysitting, and any other source of income. It is imperative that every expense and all income are recorded in this program for this to be successful.

That's it, only five minutes a day. Begin right now, even if you don't have your receipts. I'm sure you remember what you spent today and yesterday. Since you are now keeping your receipts, after inputting them into this program, put them into an envelope marked "Receipts for the Month of _____." You will find that it is very easy to organize your receipts this way and also that, if you ever need find a receipt, you will know exactly where it is. Make sure you start your *My Money* program right now before you continue.

My Money				
Date	**Amount**	**Item Description**	**Category**	**Method of Payment**
Total				

This program enables you to track purchases and locate receipts if things break or wear out. It is also great at tax time. If your accountant wants any information regarding your expenses, it is all right here. Search by category, date, amount, or method of payment—whatever is convenient for you.

> **Action Steps:**
>
> Starting today: Begin asking for a receipt and keep each one. You can download *My Money* for free at www.DreamsUnlimited.org. It is important that you begin to input your expenses daily, as it will give you a greater awareness of your income and expenses.

Knowledge is power.
Sir Francis Bacon

Chapter Fifteen

Monitoring Cash Flow

The next method is the *My Cash Flow* program. After entering your receipts and all income into *My Money,* the information will be used to create *My Cash Flow*. The *My Cash Flow* program will show you how much you have spent in each category for that month, as well as your income, and if you have spent more or less than you have earned.

Below you will find *My Cash Flow*. Because you create the categories for your expenses (e.g., dining out, groceries, etc.), *My Cash Flow* will show only what you have entered so far. You can also choose to view by month, average per month, and see year-to-date to compare your expenses and income to previous periods and better decide how you wish to continue spending your money. The following is an example of what it looks like:

Monitoring Cash Flow

My Cash Flow			
	JANUARY	TOTAL	AVERAGE
INCOME			
<u>**FIXED INCOME**</u>			
SALARY GROSS			
Person #1 (Insert Name Here)			
SUB TOTAL INCOME			
OTHER INCOME			
OTHER INCOME—Person #1			
MISCELLANEOUS INCOME			
SUBTOTAL OTHER INCOME			
TOTAL INCOME			
EXPENSES	JANUARY	TOTAL	AVERAGE
FEDERAL INCOME TAX			
SOCIAL SECURITY (FICA)			
FEDERAL MEDICARE			
TOTAL TAXES			
TOTAL NET INCOME			
<u>**FIXED EXPENSES**</u>			
MORTGAGE or RENT			
HOMEOWNERS INSURANCE			
HOME PHONE			
INTERNET			
CELL PHONE			
TV			
ELECTRICITY or GAS			
OTHER INSURANCE			
DEBT PAYMENTS (revolving balance CC)			

Monitoring Cash Flow

STUDENT LOAN PAYMENTS			
TOTAL FIXED EXPENSES			
VARIABLE EXPENSES	**JANUARY**	**TOTAL**	**AVERAGE**
GROCERIES			
DINING OUT			
CLOTHING			
ENTERTAINMENT			
TRAVEL			
FITNESS			
MOVIES			
	JANUARY	**TOTAL**	**AVERAGE**
HOME IMPROVEMENT			
BOOKS/MUSIC			
SUBSCRIPTIONS			
GIFTS			
CHARITY			
HOUSEHOLD			
GASOLINE			
CAR MAINTENANCE			
HEALTH			
MEMBERSHIPS			
TOTAL VARIABLE EXPENSES			
TOTAL EXPENSES			
LEFTOVER THIS MONTH			
LEFTOVER FROM LAST MONTH			
ACCUMULATIVE LEFTOVER			

The purpose of this program is to track your expenses and income so that you will be able to see your spending habits and exactly where your money is going. Look at and evaluate each category. Think about what is most important to you. How much do you spend on rent/mortgage, car insurance, car payments, etc...? Can you find more affordable housing, less expensive insurance; get a car that is less expensive with lower or no monthly payments?

My purpose is to empower you, to see that tomorrow can be better than today and today can be better than yesterday by making different choices. The real challenge is not in setting this up and spending five minutes a day doing it. The real challenge is in your mind. You must battle your internal wars and expand your comfort zone so that you can enjoy the reality of what you are now in the process of creating.

For best results, update *My Cash Flow* regularly. I recommend you update and view it weekly for the first two months, then monthly thereafter. This program is critical in learning your habits and where you spend your money. It is after you know where it is going that you can better choose how you want to spend it in the future.

Action Steps:

Visit www.DreamsUnlimited.org and download *My Cash Flow* for free. Every week, update the information from *My Money* into *My Cash Flow* and see where your money is going. This is one of the most important steps that you can take to begin changing your paradigm and habits about money. Seeing where your money has gone allows you to be conscious of the choices you make today about tomorrow.

---

*Money is like manure; it's not worth a
thing unless it's spread around
encouraging young things to grow.*

Thornton Wilder

PART IV

SAVING MORE

Chapter Sixteen

Pay Yourself First and
Make It Automatic

The United States government learned that the most effective way to collect taxes is to get paid first, directly from an employee's paycheck. That is why, in around 1940, Congress passed a law allowing this to take place and it has ever since.

Right now, you are probably last in a long line behind rent, credit card bills, car payment, dining out, clothes, presents, etc. That's okay, because you can be become second in line very quickly.

The reason why you don't have any money is because you spend it all hoping that when you are done spending, you will have some left over. I hate to be the one to tell you this, but whatever amount you have to spend, you will.

The most successful way of saving money is to do it first and make it automatic, just like the government has done with taxes. That is why I propose that you begin paying yourself first, and making it automatic.

That means you must create a system such as a direct deposit into a separate account for savings, or taking an amount of your paycheck and putting it somewhere where you can begin to manage this as the beginning of your wealth building process.

My Savings Account

Here is how it works. Below you will see a blank version of the *My Savings Account* system. Immediately following, will be an explanation of how to use it.

Column 1 is the priority value. One is the highest priority and indicates what is most important to you.

Column 2 is where you will write what it is that you are going to save for (e.g., vacation, computer, 60-inch flat screen TV, rainy day emergency money, etc.).

Column 3 is where you list how much you have currently saved for this goal. It is okay if it is zero right now.

Column 4 is the amount you will put toward this goal every time you receive money. Most people do this is by saving part of their paychecks. However, if you receive commissions or irregular amounts of income, then you may choose to use a percentage of your income instead of a quantity of income. I'll talk more about this in a moment.

Column 5 is the total amount you will need to realize each goal.

Column 6 is the date by which you would like to have the money in hand for your goal.

Fill out *My Savings Account* now, leaving column 4 (the amount you are going to save) blank.

Pay Yourself First and Make It Automatic

Priority	Name of Goal	Balance	$ / Paycheck	Total Needed	Due Date
	My Savings Account				
1					
2					
3					
4					
5					
6					
7					
8					
9					
10					
	Total				

Now that you have filled out you're *My Savings Account* System, you want to know how much you need to pay yourself in order to have that much money by the date you've chosen in the final column.

Click the upper portion of column 4 and choose the way in which you would like to pay yourself. You will see many options, including: every other week from paycheck, two times per month, once per month, and percentage of income. If you select percentage of income, it will ask you how much you anticipate earning, and the frequency by which you are paid. After selecting one of these options, you can select the "calculate" button at the bottom of the spreadsheet, and the amount you must pay yourself to meet your goals will automatically appear in column 4. This works for columns 3 (current balance), 4 (amount paid to self), and 6 (due date). Fill out any two of these, and by selecting "calculate" it will automatically provide you with the third piece of information.

This is very helpful in gauging how much you wish to pay yourself and how long it will take to reach your goal.

One goal I suggest you create is what I call *Cash Reserve*. This is an amount of money sitting in your account for whatever you need it for, a "rainy day fund." Your car may need new brakes and tires costing you $800 that you don't have. This is the purpose of the cash reserve. It is used only when NEEDED, not for meeting a desire of immediate gratification.

We also have one for presents. We love to give great Christmas presents, but don't always have an extra $1,000 for that. We also use this for presents throughout the year—birthdays, anniversaries, weddings, etc. By each of us saving $25 per paycheck, we can comfortably spend $1,200 per year without it even affecting our cash flow.

We love to travel, so we save $100 per paycheck in order to take a beautiful $5,000 vacation every year without going into debt. Although most people don't realize it, the money one receives for paid time off from work is usually eaten up by regular expenses that you must pay, whether you are at home or on vacation.

If you are planning on using the money from your paid time off to pay for your vacation, you are likely to end up paying for your vacation with a credit card. You will probably spend the next several years paying that off, paying double the amount your vacation actually cost, due to the high rates of interest from your credit card.

That is why we pay for our vacation in advance. It costs us about $10 per day if you break it down. That's not much to pay yourself to enjoy an amazing vacation every year.

We also have a category called "vehicles." This money goes for unexpected expensive repairs and to purchase our next vehicle. Instead of paying $300 per month to buy or lease a vehicle, pay yourself that money, or a fraction of that, and pay cash for your next car. It really is that easy. If you already have car payments, consider saving for your next car.

If you don't have a savings account set up, go to your bank and open one. Often times, your bank or credit union has money market accounts that, with a balance over $10,000, will give you a much higher rate of interest. Although your account might not be close to this amount, it certainly can be in the years to come, if you use this planning tool and begin today.

We opened a savings account with about $100 when we had very little money. Automatically saving $5, then $10, then $20, then $50, and now over $300 per week to this account, we have created the means to obtain virtually all of our financial saving goals by using *My Savings Account.*

Whenever you deposit money, or make withdrawals, you must update this system. It is only as good as it is accurate. If you take $100 from this account, you must choose which of your goals you wish to subtract the $100 from.

Once you set up *My Savings Account,* you can click on the *update now button* every payday and it will automatically update to reflect the amount that you have automatically deposited into your savings account.

Many companies offer direct deposit as an alternative to receiving a paycheck that you must deposit yourself. If possible, use the direct deposit method so that the first amount you pay is to yourself into your savings account, and the remainder goes to your regular checking account for living expenses. If you do this, it will virtually guarantee your financial success in saving for these areas. As long as you are realistic with the amount you can commit to saving regularly, this will be fun to view every payday and update with your new deposit, seeing how much closer you are to attaining your goals.

Unless you are extremely well-disciplined, I cannot stress enough the importance of making saving automatic. If you choose to do it yourself and manually deposit that amount into your savings account system, you will be tempted every time to pay yourself a little less, or a day or two later, and then postpone it until the following payday. I have seen this happen more times than I would like to admit. That is why the United States government created an automatic system that pays them first. It works.

Action Steps:

Visit www.DreamsUnlimited.org and download your free copy of *My Savings Account*. Then fill it out and review it weekly. It is important that you use this to help guide you to where you want to be.

This is not an option. I started out with $50 in a savings account in 2003, and one of my most recent statements had over $43,000. This has come from diligently paying myself first, and making it automatic, for the last five years. It may be challenging at first, like exercise, but after you are in shape, it feels so liberating.

If you cannot make money on one dollar—
if you do not coax one dollar to work hard
for you, you won't know how to make
money out of one thousand dollars.

E. S. Kinnear

Chapter Seventeen

The Value of Home Ownership

Archimedes said, *Give me a lever long enough and I shall move the world*. Leverage is how and why there is such value in home ownership.

Most likely the greatest financial investment you will ever make will be to buy your own home. There is a reason that it is such a large part of the American Dream. Home ownership gives you a certain confidence that it is permanent, yours, and nobody can take it away. That is not completely true, but it is often the feeling that accompanies moving into your first home. Whether you buy it today, in ten years or at age 75, you will begin creating ownership in your financial future.

If you choose to rent, you will be paying someone else's mortgage for the rest of your life. If you choose to buy your own home, you will be contributing to your financial future. Would you prefer to contribute to someone else's financial future by renting? Or to your financial future by buying your own home? It is that simple.

Have you ever met someone who was very wealthy who was still renting their home? Owning is a prerequisite for creating wealth. There are too many advantages and reasons why you should own your own home for you not to do so.

One major advantage is a tax deduction of all interest that you pay on your mortgage, which is over 90% of your payments the first several years of your mortgage.

The Value of Home Ownership

Often, the cost of purchasing a home is not much more than renting. You won't have to worry about a rent increase every six months, either. You can paint your walls without anyone's permission and sleep better knowing that you now have a piece of the American Dream.

You will find that housing (rent, or mortgage payments) are the greatest expense in one's total budget. If you choose to rent forever, you are choosing to always spend the greatest part of your income on housing. Should you choose to purchase a home, you can have it paid off in as little as 15-20 years and then pay only property taxes, which usually are equal to about 1% of the property value. If you owned a home valued at $300,000, your property taxes would be about $3,000 per year or $250 per month. After your house is paid off, your monthly housing budget would only be $250 (or its future equivalent with inflation).

Your mortgage payment won't change if you have a fixed 30-year loan. If your monthly payment is $1,000 per month, it will never change if you choose a fixed-interest-rate loan. If you rent, the monthly amount will increase every time you renew your lease.

Rent can only go up; and if you're paying $1000 per month today, expect to pay $2,000 per month in ten years, and $4,000 per month in 20 years. In 20 years, would you prefer paying $1,000 per month and own your own home or $4,000 and still be renting? It's up to you.

In addition to the amount you're spending on rent, you gain nothing financially by renting. By owning your own home, you can expect an appreciation gain over time. There are no guarantees and there have always and will always be areas that have lost value, but this is rare and it is still a solid investment.

I use 6.8% as an appreciation rate. Appreciation means that your home increases in value, and is worth more with time. For fun, let's say you bought a home for $300,000 five years ago. At 6.8% (the national average of housing value growth since 1968 according the National

The Value of Home Ownership

Association of Realtors), it would now be worth $421,079. That means you have a paper gain of $121,079.

To save the same amount in a typical savings account at today's average interest rate of 0.2%, you would have to save $2,008 every month for the same five-year period! Home ownership allows you the ability to know your home value is increasing and that, every day, you are getting closer and closer to owning it completely, virtually eliminating housing from your budget.

A recent *USA Today* statistic showed that households that rent have an estimated net worth of $10,000, while the average household that owns has an average net worth of $75,000. Which category would you like to be a part of?

You can clearly see how valuable home ownership is. As long as you don't continuously take out additional loans against your equity, you will be well on your way to financial success and much closer to outright home ownership. In the book *The Millionaire Next Door*, Dr. Stanley states that millionaires tend to live in their middle class homes for 30 years or until they own it, before moving to another home. I recommend the same.

If housing takes 30% of your income, then when you retire, you could live on 30% less income if you own our own home outright. Think about that. Do you want to retire at 50, 60, or 70—or will you be able to retire at all?

Primerica (www.primerica.com) has released statistics that may encourage you to take immediate action. In 2003, roughly two million Americans declared bankruptcy. Of those retirement age, only one percent was wealthy, five percent were well off, 44% were still working, and 50% were flat broke trying to survive on social security. Only six percent of those over age 60 today in the United States are financially well off.

Begin looking at home ownership as a necessary step in your financial future. Remember, there is no better day than today to begin building for tomorrow!

Action Steps:

If you are currently renting, evaluate whether purchasing a home would be a step that would help you create greater financial well-being. How much can you afford per month in mortgage payments? How much are houses or condos going for in your area?

www.realtor.com is one of many, great online resources to search for homes in your area and find out what housing prices are. Here is a rule of thumb for determining how much your mortgage will cost:

Divide the total amount you are borrowing (the mortgage amount) by 10,000. Multiply this number by 80 and you will have an approximate amount of the cost for the principle, interest, property taxes and insurance. (*Example: a $300,000 mortgage divided by 10,000 is 30. 30 multiplied by 80 comes to $2,400 per month.*)

If you choose to move forward, I encourage you to find an experienced realtor with 10 years or more of experience, as there are few realtors who succeed over a long period of time and they are the ones who have the experience and historic wisdom to guide you in searching for your home.

If service is the rent you pay for your existence
on this earth, are you behind in your rent?
Robert G. Allen

PART V

GIVING MORE

Chapter Eighteen

Vision and Goals

Give yourself the gift of success. That starts with a goal and a commitment.

Goals are discussed in virtually all success literature. In its simplest form, a goal is a target that you are aiming for. It is a tool used by successful people to measure how they have done over a period of time. It is an excellent way to help guide your future.

Mark McCormack, in his book *What They Don't Teach You at Harvard Business School,* tells of a Harvard study conducted between 1979 and 1989. In 1979, the graduates of the MBA program at Harvard were asked, "Have you set clear, written goals for your future and made plans to accomplish them?" It turned out that only 3% of the graduates had written goals and plans. Thirteen percent had goals, but they were not in writing. Eighty-four percent had no specific goals at all, aside from getting out of school and enjoying the summer.

Ten years later, in 1989, the researchers interviewed the members of that class again. They found that the 13% who had goals that were not in writing were earning, on average, twice as much as the 84% of graduates who had no goals at all. But, more surprisingly, they found that the 3% of graduates who had clear, written goals when they left Harvard were earning, on average, ten times as much as the other 97% of graduates all together. The only difference between the groups was the clarity of the goals they had for themselves when they graduated.

Vision and Goals

As this study shows, goals are an essential part of planning for success. As the saying goes, "People do not plan to fail, they fail to plan." This is the most accurate way I can explain that you cannot get to a destination without first deciding what that destination will be. Have you ever driven a car blindfolded or boarded a plane not knowing where you were going? Why would you leave your life up to chance when you can be in the driver's seat?

Becoming debt free, building a savings account with six months of reserves, owning our own home, and going on extended international vacations were not something that happened for us overnight. We created them from our vision and goals, some long-term and some short-term. We broke down the goal of having $3,000 to go on vacation into small manageable goals in which, from every paycheck, we each put $58 into our savings account. In 12 months, we got on a plane and spent a month in South America. It was that simple.

Notice, I did not say *easy*. Although it may have been simple, it was challenging at first to have $58 automatically deposited into our savings account every payday. However, this was something that we learned to cope with and, in a month, we forgot that we ever had the money in the first place.

Goals are the building blocks on which success is created. The following is my preferred definition of success, provided by Earl Nightingale:

Success is the progressive realization
of a worthy goal or ideal.

Creating goals requires vision, a vision of what you intend to create. Vision is the first step toward determining a destination. This vision must be powerful, provide passion and a drive for you to reach it. Vision is the first step and, often times, the part that dissipates or fades with adversity.

Vision and Goals

There are no restrictions on what children dream of becoming someday. They want to be doctors, firemen, *National Geographic* photographers, scuba divers—anything they can imagine that they believe with all their heart that they can and will achieve.

Do you remember when the dreams began to fade in your life? Were you the last one picked for sports teams in school (rejection and failure)? As you grew up, was your heart broken (again, rejection and failure)? Maybe you didn't do as well academically as you needed to, to get into the University of your Dreams (more rejection and failure). Then the company you really wanted to work for hired someone else (more rejection and failure). Maybe your marriage did not last (more rejection and failure). Life can be a continual experience of rejection and failure, but your attitude toward life is what will determine if you keep that vision alive—that vision of the small child who believed that the world was completely cooperative and would allow his/her dreams to be realized.

Thomas Edison did not fail thousands of times in making an incandescent light bulb. He said that every attempt to create the incandescent light that was not successful, taught him one more way not to do it the next time. It was his "failures" that created his success.

Walt Disney, as a young man, was fired for his lack of creativity. He maintained an attitude strong enough to keep his vision alive and continue to progressively realize his worthy goals.

Goal Setting

I have found that breaking up large projects such as goal setting is often the most effective way to proceed. The first part is creating a vision. This may be a vision of your life from which you will derive many goals; or perhaps you may choose to have many different visions that are more specific to each goal. Vision is the beginning, the foundation of goal setting. Before one can chart the course, the destination must be identified.

After you have a clear vision, creatively bring it to life by drawing, painting, building a model, making a collage from magazines, or simply writing down your vision in as much detail as possible. The more accurate and detailed you are, the more precise you can be in creating goals that will help you realize this vision.

After you have a clear vision that excites you when you think about it, you are ready for the next step, charting the course. It is much like driving across the country. When I drove from Seattle to Miami, I didn't just start driving. I charted a course, choosing which destinations I wanted to stop at along the way, which freeways I would take, where I would spend the night, visit friends and family. My course was not a straight line—and our lives rarely are; but I did reach each destination city and arrive in Miami, my ultimate destination.

Begin with the end in mind and move backward. The reason the first step is so challenging is we often don't know what it is. Working backward has helped me tremendously in determining if my goals are realistic and attainable. Have you ever set a high expectation or goal for yourself and then didn't even come close to accomplishing it? That is my weakness, aiming too high. It is important to set the bar high, but not so high that you don't give yourself the opportunity to get close.

A method I have found to be quite useful is known as SMART goal setting. It is an acronym: Specific, Measurable, Achievable, Relative, and Time-bound. When creating goals, I use this method as it helps me ensure that the goal will be actually achievable. Remember, the purpose of the goal is 1) to achieve it, and 2) to saturate it with enough visual and emotional ties to create the motivation to achieve it.

Specific refers to the specificity of the goal, i.e. *I will be debt free.* It is important that the goal be specific so that you know exactly what you are going toward. Generic—such as *I will be rich* or *I will no longer live paycheck to paycheck*—does not work here.

Measurable refers to how the goal will be measured. If the goal is specific enough, it is most likely measurable; e.g., *I will be debt free....* This can be measured by the degree by which you are debt free. If you have paid off 95% of your debt by the date set in your goal, you have achieved 95% of your goal. Celebrate the success and pay off the last 5%. Smaller goals or action steps are often required to obtain each goal.

Achievable refers to the degree by which the goal is obtainable. I am the master of getting excited and setting unrealistic expectations that are not achievable. In the end, I set myself up for failure when I do not accomplish my goal and then beat myself up for not reaching the bar that was set way too high. So make sure the goal is a stretch, but not stressful. Goals should be in the stretch zone, not in the stress zone. Achieving goals will create momentum and you can increase their difficulty as you get more comfortable accomplishing them. An example of such an achievable goal would be: *I will have saved $1,000 in my savings account by September 31, 2009.*

Relative refers to whether or not it pertains to your vision. Is this a worthy goal? Remember the definition of *success* we referred to earlier: *"Success is the progressive realization of a worthy goal."* Make sure your goal is in alignment with your vision. If the vision is to have greater wealth, security, time with family, time to work out, eat healthier, travel more, etc., then a goal of becoming debt free would be very relative to this vision.

Time Bound refers to the date set for the actualization of the goal. A goal without a date is wishful thinking. If there is no date, it is highly unlikely it will ever occur, as it is a loophole the subconscious uses to allow you to work on it indefinitely with little to no results. I prefer an exact date; e.g., *I will have made my last payment and be debt free on or before March 19, 2010.*

Vision and Goals

Over and over in my life, I have set goals, visualized their realization and worked toward their attainment. I will share one such story with you.

Years ago, I was dissatisfied at work and wanted a change. I sat down one evening and wrote a list of 13 items that I wanted to manifest professionally. These included doubling the amount of money I earned, having greater freedom and flexibility in my work and contributing more profoundly to the people with whom I worked. I forgot about this list and, six months later, received an email with the scenario I had manifested. This email was an opportunity to work as a Trainer in the Marketing and Training Department, training all internal employees in the company. I eagerly applied for the position and went through the interview process. Three months later, I was chosen to be the new Trainer for the company. One month after starting my new position, I found the original list that I had made and counted 12 of the 13 items I had written down that had been realized in my new position. This would not have been possible without first having had a vision and desire, and writing down exactly what I wanted. My dreams literally became reality in only six months.

I share this story because that which we desire, think about, concentrate on, and ask for will be found in greater abundance.

Whatever we believe and put out into the Universe comes back to us, often in ways we do not expect. The challenge is often recognizing the opportunity when it comes in camouflaged form. From these opportunities, we have choices and those choices will lead to where we find ourselves tomorrow.

It starts right now with your goals and your commitment. Complete the following commitment to yourself and then take your first step toward that goal, no matter how small the step.

Vision and Goals

I, _____, hereby fully commit my complete intention to:

    1. _____ on or

       before _____.

    2. _____ on or

       before _____.

    3. _____ on or

       before _____.

Signed: _____.

Today's Date: _____.

Action Steps:

In addition to completing the above commitment of intention, review your collage from Chapter 5 and add to it, if you feel there are areas yet to be explored.

Shoot for the moon. Even if you miss,
you'll land among the stars.

Les Brown

Chapter Nineteen

Giving Back, Spiritual Magic

There is an invisible force I call *spiritual magic.* The more I give of what I want to have, the more I find it in greater abundance in my life. Whether it is love, smiles, money, time, or energy, I find that every time I give it away, it comes back in greater and greater abundance.

All great people provide something to others. Bill Gates, co-founder and former CEO of Microsoft, employed over 100,000 people and his Foundation helps millions worldwide. Ted Turner committed several billion dollars to the United Nations, and asked others fortunate to be blessed financially to do the same.

What is *giving back?* Donating to your favorite charities, your church? Giving back means different things to different people, but to me it is a relationship and an experience. Why does every book on financial success suggest that you give back part of your hard-earned income?

Imagine if today every American would give $0.25 toward ending poverty on the planet. That would be $75,000,000, enough to purchase three million cups of uncooked rice, which would feed about one billion people for a day. We could feed 20% of the entire world's population by donating 25 cents. This would cost every American about $8.00 per month. I don't know about you, but I would be willing to go without a double-shot-venti-soy-hazelnut-vanilla-cinnamon-white-mocha-with-extra-white-mocha-and-caramel (estimated cost, $6.00), to feed somebody for a month.

Giving Back, Spiritual Magic

The power of using one's resources to help the world elevate its well-being cannot be underestimated. But giving back does not have to be in a monetary form.

Making a difference can be simply starting in your neighborhood, city, state, country, or the world. We must give back that which is most difficult. For some, that is time—to volunteer (at a food bank, or your children's school); for others, it is money.

Frequently, what we want most is what we have least. For example, we want more time when we feel our days are overfilled with commitments. We desire more money when we feel we don't have enough of it. But when we give freely that which we want most, without the expectation of receiving anything in return, the universe will deliver to us our desired gifts in abundance.

Last Christmas, my wife and I decided to give a friend who was in great need $250.00. We did this as a gift with no strings attached. We felt so grateful that we could make a difference in someone's life, and it was as much a gift to us as it was to her.

Two weeks later, the fireplace repairman showed up to repair our pilot light that I could not keep lit despite my numerous attempts to repair it myself. The cost was going to be about $250.00. The nice young man fixed the pilot light in less than two minutes and said that there would be no charge. Though I offered to pay, he declined anything I offered him. I didn't think about it until later, but the $250.00 that we had so willingly given only 14 days earlier had just found its way back into our lives.

Starting in 2006, for Christmas we have chosen to inform our friends, co-workers, and neighbors that instead of giving them gifts that they probably didn't want anyway, we would do something to make a difference in the world.

We searched for families who experienced financial challenge, and gave our money to them so that they could provide their children with a great Christmas—including a Christmas tree, presents, and a holiday meal. We have never felt better and didn't have to wander the malls looking for the "co-worker gifts" that everyone ends up re-gifting, anyway.

We attempt to gather as much information about the joy these gifts bring to their recipients and share that with our friends and family, sometimes as an email, or more formal presentation with photos. The joy of contribution cannot be overstated.

In November 2008, I received a phone call from an organization I was affiliated with asking if we would like to donate our time or money to helping the organization help financially-challenge families. I eagerly said yes, and told them I had been looking for such an organization since it was difficult to do it by ourselves. Every year at Christmas, I now encourage all of my friends and family to think about the holidays and the experience they want to have. If they feel inclined, I invite them to take part in making a difference—and what a great gift for your children to see how wonderful it is to help others.

There is great power in giving back. When we give from a true sense of love, we feel that we have enough to provide for others. This is an abundance paradigm, and when we continue to follow the principles of this paradigm, the universe provides for us in ways we cannot imagine. Because there is plenty, we, too, are rewarded with more; and because we feel grateful, we give from a sense of true stewardship. This is a cycle that can continue indefinitely. We must take that first step toward stewardship and give of ourselves. It must be done in a generous nature, so as to create a paradigm of abundance.

This is true wealth, the ability to make a difference in the world. The greater your paradigm of abundance, the greater your ability is to contribute. The true power and freedom in giving is liberating and humbling. It is a requirement of greater financial well-being.

Part of my vision is using the abundance created through Dreams Unlimited to help elevate the well-being of humanity. That is why 10% of every dollar that comes into this organization will be spent in a philanthropic nature.

I encourage you to fill out the following commitment to yourself and begin giving that which you want most.

I, _____, hereby fully commit my complete intention to:

4. _____ on or

    before _____.

5. _____ on or

    before _____.

6. _____ on or

    before _____.

Signed: _____.

Today's Date: _____.

Action Steps:

In addition to completing the above commitment of intention, I encourage you to review the action steps, your notes, and journaling pages. Review the programs you downloaded from www.DreamsUnlimited.org and commit to maintaining them in addition to keeping your vision for your future alive! Keep on using DreamsUnlimited.org as a resource for your continued success.

The real measure of your wealth
is how much you'd be worth if
you lost all your money.

Unknown

Chapter Twenty

Leading by Example, Living a Purposeful Life

The greatest experience in life is to live abundantly doing what one loves. All truly successful people have both of these in their lives. Doing what they love, they never feel like they are working and, therefore, never wish away any part of their life for the weekend or the vacation or the fishing trip. Living a purposeful life is the ultimate way to lead by example, demonstrating to those around you the potential that exists when we truly live our lives with passion.

One of my favorite quotations from Gandhi is, *"My life is my message"*. He lived his life every day as if it were how he wanted the world to be. He also said, *"Be the change you want in the world."*

We cannot all be Gandhi, but we can learn from him and the thousands of others who have lived purposeful lives and continue to live as an example for others to follow.

I encourage you to review this text and redo the exercises often, as if you had never done them before. Try new things in life. Tomorrow when you go to work, take a different route. Kiss your husband or wife a little more passionately, smile more, and remember: You are in control of your life. The choices you make right now will provide you with results tomorrow. Decide today what results you want and take action. Taking action immediately after you set a goal is ten times more likely to be accomplished.

I hope that you have found this book to be educational, informative, entertaining, inspiring, and motivating. Please continue to use the systems and programs available at www.DreamsUnlimited.org, as they will be the foundation that will help you achieve the financial well-being you desire and deserve.

I leave you with a favorite quotation of mine from Ralph Waldo Emerson:

> *What lies behind you and what lies*
> *before you pale insignificant with*
> *what lies within you.*

I wish you all the best as you create greater financial well-being in your life. It is now in your hands.

Appendix I

Filling Out *My Savings Account* by Hand

If you will be doing *My Savings Account* manually without the use of a computer, you will need to calculate some of the categories yourself. Follow these simple steps:

1. Write the name of your goal under the "Name of Goal" column.
2. Write how much money you have already saved for this goal—or $0.00 if you have not yet begun saving for this—under the "Balance" column.
3. Write the total amount you think you will need under the "Total Needed" column.
4. Write how much you wish to save per paycheck under the "$/Paycheck" column.
5. The final column, "Due Date," will require doing some math. Divide the total needed by the amount you will save from each paycheck. The number will be the total number of paychecks it will take for you to save for this goal. Now, depending on how many paychecks you have per month, you can figure out how long it will be from today until you have saved the total amount needed for this goal. Write down the date (or round to the nearest month) in the "Due Date" column.
6. Repeat these steps for each goal.

Appendix II

The Five Charts

My Financial Statement			
Assets		**Liabilities**	
Description	**Value**	**Description**	**Value**
Total Asset Value		**Total Liabilities Value**	
Current Net Worth			

My Debt Freedom: The Hybrid Stacking Method					
Rank	**Debt owed to**	**Amount Owed**	**Interest Rate**	**Minimum Payment/Mo.**	**Debt- Free Date**

My Money				
Date	Amount	Item Description	Category	Method of Payment
Total				

My Savings Account					
Priority	Name of Goal	Balance	$ / Paycheck	Total Needed	Due Date
1					
2					
3					
4					
5					
6					
7					
8					
9					
10					
	Total				

My Cash Flow			
	JANUARY	TOTAL	AVERAGE
INCOME			
<u>**FIXED INCOME**</u>			
SALARY GROSS			
Person #1 (Insert Name Here)			
SUB TOTAL INCOME			
OTHER INCOME			
OTHER INCOME—Person #1			
MISCELLANEOUS INCOME			
SUBTOTAL OTHER INCOME			
TOTAL INCOME			
EXPENSES	JANUARY	TOTAL	AVERAGE
FEDERAL INCOME TAX			
SOCIAL SECURITY (FICA)			
FEDERAL MEDICARE			
TOTAL TAXES			
TOTAL NET INCOME			
<u>**FIXED EXPENSES**</u>			
MORTGAGE or RENT			
HOMEOWNERS INSURANCE			
HOME PHONE			
INTERNET			
CELL PHONE			
TV			
ELECTRICITY or GAS			
OTHER INSURANCE			

STUDENT LOAN PAYMENTS			
TOTAL FIXED EXPENSES			
VARIABLE EXPENSES			
GROCERIES	**JANUARY**	**TOTAL**	**AVERAGE**
DINING OUT			
CLOTHING			
ENTERTAINMENT			
TRAVEL			
FITNESS			
MOVIES			
HOME IMPROVEMENT	**JANUARY**	**TOTAL**	**AVERAGE**
BOOKS/MUSIC			
SUBSCRIPTIONS			
GIFTS			
CHARITY			
HOUSEHOLD			
GASOLINE			
CAR MAINTENANCE			
HEALTH			
MEMBERSHIPS			
TOTAL VARIABLE EXPENSES			
TOTAL EXPENSES			
LEFTOVER THIS MONTH			
LEFTOVER FROM LAST MONTH			
ACCUMULATIVE LEFTOVER			

Dreams Unlimited Website

The Dreams Unlimited website offers great value to all visitors. Whether you are reading the blog, checking the schedule for upcoming classes in your area, downloading the free financial programs, or enjoying the resource section, there is something for everyone. –The objective of our website is to be the conduit for communication and learning opportunities.

Our intention is to continue creating value for our members and all visitors to the site. This comes in many forms including streaming audio and video as well as downloadable versions to watch at your convenience. We invite you to visit, take a tour, and drop us a line. The following pages will provide greater detail into some of the many opportunities our website has to offer. Enjoy!

www.dreamsunlimited.org

2274 Newport Way NW ▪ Issaquah WA 98027 ▪ 206.817.3286

FINANCIAL TRANSFORMATION

A Journey to Financial Well-Being

This book is changing lives by telling the story of a generation in debt. Simple solutions to complex financial challenges help define what is truly most important and how to create and execute a plan to move in the direction of one's dreams.

It is written clearly and simply, yet carries a profound message what can happen when one chooses to live an awakened life, consciously and deliberately choosing which path to take.

Readers are calling *A Journey to Financial Well-Being* a great financial foundation for individuals, families, and businesses. One's relationship with money is developed at an early age and seldom changes throughout life. The subject of money is not taught in schools, and rare is the family that passes on healthy financial habits. The reason that 9 in 10 people and 9 in 10 businesses fail financially can be learned from the fundamental principles in this book; people don't know that they are a business and do not operate like one. Learn how to create a healthier relationship with money by taking an active role in your life and reading *A Journey to Financial well-Being* today.

FINANCIAL TRANSFORMATION

The e-book of *A Journey to Financial Well-Being* is now available on our website. It is offered in a new format 8 ½ by 11. It can be downloaded within minutes and is offered at only half the price of the paperback version. Great for immediate access; those who wish to read it on their computer, or print it out for greater readability. It is available for purchase at our online bookstore at

www.dreamsunlimited.org

Sign up to receive e-newsletter!

We want to give you information that will benefit you and create greater financial well-being in your life. That is exactly what you will find in the exclusive Dreams Unlimited newsletter available for a limited time absolutely free. Simply visit our website, and sign up for the Journey newsletter.

DREAMS UNLIMITED
Where Dreams Come Alive

www.dreamsunlimited.org

2274 Newport Way NW ■ Issaquah WA 98027 ■ 206.817.3286

FINANCIAL TRANSFORMATION

The Dreams Unlimited Blog is devoted to providing you valuable information on a regular basis, from ways to save money, to informative articles, from interviews to fun things to do with your family. The purpose of our blog is to provide you with fun, valuable, and pertinent information to help you experience greater fulfillment. You can find it on our website at www.dreamsunlimited.org.

The Dreams Unlimited website has valuable resources for you under the *resources tab*. There you will find Recommended:

- Seminars
- Websites
- Speakers
- Books
- Movies
- Quotations

www.dreamsunlimited.org

2274 Newport Way NW ■ Issaquah WA 98027 ■ 206.817.3286

FINANCIAL TRANSFORMATION

Classes

The Pillars of Financial Well-Being

This class is fun, interactive, fast paced and prepares you to begin taking action before you leave.

This is a companion to the book, *A Journey to Financial Well-Being*. In this exciting class you will have the opportunity to see Jesse live, speak about his experience, share the pillars of financial well-being and walk you through each of the programs that are in his book.

The class is for anyone who wants to get out of debt, old enough to have a bank account, anyone who wishes to retire someday, anyone who wants more of the good things in life, and anyone who wants more out of life.

Debt-Free Forever, is the second class offered by Dreams Unlimited, and is expressly for those who have finally had enough and want to shed the debt once and for all. Learn not only how to get out of debt, but more importantly how to stay out! This class is taught by Jesse Hartman and you can sign up through our website www.dreamsunlimited.org or by calling us at 206.817.3286

Debt-Free Forever

www.dreamsunlimited.org

2274 Newport Way NW ■ Issaquah WA 98027 ■ 206.817.3286

FINANCIAL TRANSFORMATION

Also available on our website are the *free downloadable programs* from this book including:

My Financial Statement

This is a system used to view your bottom line. If you added up everything you have of value and then paid off all of your debts, the number you would have is your net worth. It is recommended to use this as one of your first steps, as it will be helpful to see where you are currently, as well as track your progress over time when you update it in the future.

My Money

This important program is where expenses are entered and through *My Cash Flow* view your cash flow and financial trends.

My Cash Flow

This is an essential program that will allow you to view the flow of money that comes in and goes out of your household. First see *My Money* as it is a prerequisite to this program.

My Debt Freedom

This is one of the most effective programs to organize debts, create a plan, and take action to once and for all, get out of debt and stay out! The instructions for use can be found in the book *A Journey to Financial Well Being*.

My Savings Account

Do you remember your first savings account as a child? I had more money in mine at age 10 than I did at 20 until I created a program to begin saving for what I really wanted. Use this program to finally begin automatically paying yourself first. Read more about it in the book, *A Journey to Financial Well Being*, available here.

www.dreamsunlimited.org

2274 Newport Way NW ■ Issaquah WA 98027 ■ 206.817.3286